FRESH FOOD FAST

FRESH FOOD FAST

DELICIOUS, SEASONAL VEGETARIAN
MEALS IN UNDER AN HOUR

PETER BERLEY
and MELISSA CLARK

WILLIAM MORROW
An Imprint of HarperCollinsPublishers

also by PETER BERLEY

THE MODERN VEGETARIAN KITCHEN

A hardcover edition of this book was published in 2004 by ReganBooks

HarperCollins books may be purchased for educational, business, or sales promotional use. For information please write: Special Markets Department, HarperCollins Publishers, 10 East 53rd Street, New York, NY 10022.

FIRST WILLIAM MORROW PAPERBACK EDITION PUBLISHED 2013.

DESIGNED BY MICHELLE ISHAY
PHOTOGRAPHS BY QUENTIN BACON

The Library of Congress has cataloged the hardcover edition as follows:

Berley, Peter.
    Fresh food fast : delicious, seasonal vegetarian meals in under an hour / Peter Berley and Melissa Clark.
      p. cm.
    Includes index.
    ISBN 0-06-051514-7
    1. Vegetarian cookery. 2. Quick and easy cookery. 3. Menus. I. Clark, Melissa. II. Title.

TX837.B4778 2004
641.5'636—dc21

2003046776

ISBN 978-0-06-051515-7

13 14 15 16 17 ❖/RRD 10 9 8 7 6 5 4 3 2 1

To the sweetest cherries in my bowl:

Meggan Lee,

Kayla Jo, and

Emma Jean

For years I have received unwavering support for this book from the following friends, family, and colleagues.

Thanks to my father, **DAN BERLEY,** my biggest fan, for his encouragement, enthusiasm, and love. To my dear friend **MELISSA CLARK,** writer, for her thirst for adventure, sensitive palate, nerves of steel, and ear for the truth. To my agent **JANIS DONNAUD,** for her wisdom, care, and love for this book, and for being patient with me through all of my *mishegas*. To chef **PAUL VANDEWOUDE** and **MARIETTE BERMOWITZ** of the Miette Culinary Studio in New York City for graciously lending me the use of their cozy kitchen to test and offer classes in cooking fresh food fast. To **CASSIE JONES,** my editor, for immediately seeing the need for this book. To **QUENTIN BACON,** photographer, dream catcher, and all-around mellow dude. I was dreading the photo shoots, but Quentin made it all easy. To **ALLISON ATTENBOROUGH** for food and prop styling. To **MICHELLE ISHAY,** dear friend and gifted art director, who brings her vision of beauty and light to every page. To Judith Regan, Kurt Andrews, Tom Wengelewski, and Adrienne Makowski.

CONTENTS

Introduction. 1

Tips for Using This Book 5

Pantry. 6

Equipment 10

Spring Menus 18

Summer Menus 82

Autumn Menus 152

Winter Menus. 218

Index. 286

INTRODUCTION

Stylish, sophisticated, home-cooked meals without a fuss—is that too much to ask for? I don't think so.

One of the greatest challenges facing modern humankind is the extinction of home-cooked meals and family dining. *Fresh Food Fast* defies this trend, offering you practical meal plans with style and substance. *Fresh Food Fast* is about cosmopolitan dining that is sustainable over time. It provides straightforward instructions for simple, seasonal meals that can be prepared in under an hour. *Fresh Food Fast* is about beautiful dishes with concentrated flavors that complement one another and offer great energy.

For more than twenty years I have earned my daily bread as a chef in restaurant kitchens, caterer in private homes, and teacher in cooking schools. As a devoted husband and father, I have maintained my habit of cooking fresh, healthy meals for my family on a daily basis. This book demonstrates my super time-saving techniques and strategies for putting real food on the table fast.

These healthy, quick meals are dominated by foods that are relatively low on the food chain. All are composed of traditional, time-tested sources of nourishment, including grains, legumes, seasonal vegetables and fruits, and moderate amounts of high-quality dairy products. These meals are simple yet sophisticated, seasoned with real sea salt, fresh herbs and spices, and traditionally produced vegetable oils, wine, citrus juices, and vinegar. They are substantial and delightful fare for vegetarians and omnivores alike. And they add up to a cuisine that will satisfy friends and family members who crave home-cooked food that is honest, straightforward, and delicious, and does not overwork the cook.

Generations of epicures interested in the simple pleasures of homemade meals have known and understood the value of time-saving techniques and the thrifty use of ingredients. Traditional cultures around the world have been sustaining themselves with a steady flow of daily menus that both energize and create intimacy and vitality for thousands of years, long before the advent of restaurants, delis, and gourmet take-out shops. Working people everywhere have understood the value and convenience of bread, rice, dried corn products, beans, noodles, and pastas. These staffs of life are the foundations for a wealth of quick soups, hearty stews, zesty salads, and filling main courses. Fresh, locally grown produce—simply prepared with a minimum of fuss—contributes color, texture, and flavor. Condiments, pickles, and fermented and preserved foods—made with just sea salt, unrefined vinegar, and lactic acid cultures—add relish and contribute to good digestion and overall enjoyment. Sea vegetables are an important source of protein and minerals. The milk of goats, sheep, and cows can be cultured with complex wild yeast and bacteria to create convenient sources of highly digestible proteins, fats, and minerals with terrific flavor. There is a connection among freshness, health, convenience, and flavor that has been lost in our culture.

Fast food is nothing new. What is new is the alarming growth of centralized, corporately controlled agribusiness and livestock breeding. Highly refined, synthetic, and overprocessed foods create and feed the addictive cravings of a hedonistic and spiritually bankrupt culture that is stripped of the traditional means to nourish itself. Our culture is losing its connection to the earth and its seasonal cycles of change. By selecting healthy, natural foods and cooking them on a daily basis, we can and will enhance our lives and the lives of all creatures, plants, and organisms. As a teacher, caterer, and father, I have seen the need for *Fresh Food Fast* among my students, employers, and family.

I teach on average twenty-five to thirty public classes and fifteen to twenty private classes per year. I cater upscale dinner parties regularly, cook for my family, and write a cooking column for a major magazine. The greatest challenges I face as a cook both professionally and personally are staying inspired and dealing with severe time limitations. For inspiration I read cookbooks, go to interesting restaurants, and stay in touch with the changing seasons by frequenting green markets. Making time to visit several small family-owned farms and orchards keeps me excited about what I do, and about the people and places that make it possible. Friends who own bakeries share their bread-baking wisdom with me. These are the experiences that fill me with passion for cooking and sharing food. I am lucky.

But even with all this fabulous experience and awareness of food, nothing much can come of it without an understanding of how to craft food. Knowing the right tools and techniques to use is essential for getting dinner on the table amid the unrelenting, high-speed, material life most of us lead. For most modern humans raised in the developed world and cut off from family culinary traditions, the crucial strategy and conceptual framework that this kind of cooking entails are very hard to obtain.

Through my observations of people and their approach to food over the course of my career, I have identified three kinds of cooks: In the first group are those who possess great technical prowess, without regard for the well-being of those they feed, or for Mother Earth. These technocrats are able to execute meals without heart. They are dangerous, highly trained professionals: nutritionists, fast-food-chain workers, large-scale manufacturers and marketers and laboratory technicians employed by multinational corporations with ties to genetically engineered seed patenting, pesticide production, and animal factories. They view food only as fuel and a source of profit.

The second group includes well-intentioned cooks who care about and have a connection with the health and happiness of the earth and those they cook for, but lack skill. These cooks usually end up overwhelmed in the kitchen and unsatisfied at the table.

Finally, there are the few who cook with heart and mind. Savvy, sophisticated cooks who know how to smell a melon, where to buy the best organic staples, and how to put dinner on the table with plenty of energy to spare.

Fresh Food Fast is about how to become the third kind of cook.

When something is fresh it is new, unspoiled, pure, and full of vitality. It has real character. Freshness is something you can taste; it's an energy that feels good. Time determines freshness. It's a matter of how much time elapses between when something is produced and when it reaches the table. So the closer the cook is to the origin of the food, the better. The foods that will always have the most style and substance are the freshest, prepared in the simplest ways. A good cook can unlock the sometimes hidden qualities of fresh foods, and present meals that retain all the flavor and nourishment these foods have to offer, for us to enjoy.

Everybody knows, or certainly should be aware by now, that the average American supper consists of too much meat, poultry,

and starch. The fast, convenient, and "nutritional" food model that we are taught relegates vegetables, legumes, and grains to boring side dishes and completely misses out on seasonal diversity. (Behold the ubiquitous tossed salad, which is served, unvaried, year-round, coast to coast.)

Cooking fresh food fast comes down to context, techniques, tools, and strategy. This book addresses the essential problem that most of my students have in common: How to cook with style, have fun, and enjoy delicious meals in real time.

As a professional chef I left the restaurant business to teach and to cater small, sophisticated parties. Most people experience my cooking in a class or at a dinner party, for which I spend time to create and present seasonal dishes that can be quite involved. Of course I have the help of several kitchen assistants, who do much of the prep work and cleanup. In my work, there are three questions that students and clients inevitably ask me: The first is "Who does the cooking at home?" When I reply "I do," I can almost see the next one forming in their mind: "Well, do you eat this way every night?" My answer is "Hardly ever." And neither do any of my professional colleagues. Then comes the last and hardest question to answer, and perhaps the most important one: "Well, what do you eat at home when you are not working?"

This last question usually stumps me because it takes time to explain. First, it isn't so much what I eat as what my frame of mind is when I enter my small, low-tech, assistantless kitchen. (I do not even have the benefit of the modern mechanical equivalent of one: the dishwasher.) Second, it is what I do not cook that is important here. I do not cook in more than one stage, so I would not make a marinade, marinate some tempeh in it, roast it, then add it to a stew and simmer it for an hour. I rarely make anything that requires stuffing, so I would not sauté aromatic vegetables, cook a grain, combine it with the vegetables to make a stuffing, steam winter squash halves, fill them with stuffing, and bake them. Whoa, way too much time! I never make complicated casseroles from scratch. Just the thought of one can give me a headache. Fresh pasta? Fuggedabowdit— my hand-cranked pasta machine gets dusted off only occasionally, when I want to impress my friends or fictitious Italian in-laws (of course I love my own fresh pasta, it's just that I have so little time outside of work to cook!). Desserts have to be quick and simple or I pass. Sautéed plums with store-bought vanilla ice cream? Yes. Fresh cherry pie with a lattice crust? No way. Cook extra portions for the freezer—are you kidding? The only things in my freezer are breads, nuts, ice cream, and the occasional stock, when I have time on a weekend. Do I make fancy terrines or cute individual-size appetizers? Leap years only, pal.

So what *do* I cook? Follow me through the seasons, and try my recipes for soups and stews; breads with and in everything imaginable; savory substantial sauces and ragus for pasta and whole grains; main course salads; tons of vegetables—sautéed, steamed, panfried, roasted, baked, or raw; fruits in salads and desserts, both cooked and raw; tofu, tempeh, and seitan; eggs in omelets, frittatas, or salads; and cheeses and yogurt.

And, finally, how do I cook? How am I able to put fresh, satisfying, simple meals on my family's table night after night? Dishes as beautiful to behold as they are delicious to eat? The answer lies in every single menu. Unlike most other cookbooks, which give only recipes, my book of menus gives the reader a peek into the kitchen of a committed and professional fast, fresh cook. Every single menu in this book has a step-by-step game plan that shows you how to seamlessly orchestrate the whole meal, with instructions for each recipe, and tips on how to combine the prepping steps so the recipes are quicker and easier to put together than they would be if made separately. This is how I cook to save time, and if you follow the instructions, you will too. And this is what *Fresh Food Fast* is all about.

TIPS FOR USING THIS BOOK

To make the most of this book, read through your chosen menu before you start cooking, approaching it as if it were a single recipe. For example, if you need to cut onions for two different dishes in the same menu, cut them at the same time. The game plans that precede the recipes let you know the most efficient sequence of events.

If you are not skilled with a knife (and I strongly recommend taking a knife skills class if you're not), you should use a food processor to help cut and shred vegetables. It really speeds things up, especially in recipes like these, which use a lot of fresh vegetables.

Other timesaving techniques, such as using a single pot of boiling water to blanch vegetables before cooking pasta and pressure-cooking pulses (dried legumes such as lentils, chickpeas, fava beans, and dried peas) and grains instead of cooking them in conventional pots, are suggested throughout the book. Once you've started using them for these recipes, you'll find you start to apply these quick techniques to all the food you cook. And your meals will be faster for it.

Though fresh is undeniably the best, I do call for canned products such as tomatoes when fresh ones aren't in season or when it will really save you time, for example canned beans. When shopping for canned foods, look for the highest quality organic product. Try to cook seasonally, buying produce at its peak. It will actually save time (and money), since you'll be able to find your ingredients easily. And it will definitely taste best!

PANTRY

"The key to simple, fast cooking is magnificent, fresh ingredients whose flavors can virtually stand on their own without a cook's intervention." —Pierre Franey

BEANS, CANNED

The recipes in this book were tested with organic Eden brand canned beans. They are not at all overcooked or mushy, and contain no salt or preservatives. I like to refresh them by simmering them in lightly salted water for several minutes. Warmed beans soak up the flavors of a dish more easily. Eden also packs its products in enamel-lined cans, so the beans won't absorb any metal.

CHEESES, GRATING

Grating cheeses used to accent these recipes include Parmesan, pecorino, Grana Padano, and Asiago. Experiment with them all to experience their slightly different flavors. I think Parmesan is the most versatile of the grating cheeses. Aside from adding its own taste, it really brings out the flavor in foods in a unique way—it's a seasoning, not just a cheese.

CITRUS

Freshly squeezed citrus is far more intense and flavorful than bottled juice. You will get the most juice out of your citrus fruits if they are at room temperature. Rolling them on the counter before cutting and juicing will break down their cell structure and cause the fruit to release even more juice. Fresh citrus zest adds concentrated scent and flavor to foods in the form of the fruit's essential oil.

GRAINS

Polished grains cook more quickly than whole grains but lack the healthy bran layer. Luckily, there are now some grains on the market that fall between whole and polished. Grano (peeled wheat berries) and farro (also called spelt) are two semipolished grains that still retain a lot of the B vitamins found in whole grains. The gross outer bran layer has been removed, so they cook faster and are more digestible than whole grains. Remember to store your grains and grain products in a dark, dry, cool place, since they contain oils and have the potential to become rancid.

HERBS

I encourage you to use fresh herbs as much as possible, but if they are unavailable, you can substitute dried. Keep in mind that dried herbs have more concentrated flavor than fresh, so use about a third less when substituting crumbled dried herbs for chopped fresh ones. To dry herbs such as thyme, rosemary, or sage, just spread them out on a cookie rack (or any place where air can circulate) for a couple of days. Once the leaves are completely dry, strip them off and store them in a jar in a dark place. To keep fresh herbs, put them in a glass of water as soon as you get them home. Cover the bunch loosely with a plastic bag and store in the fridge. Hardy herbs such as rosemary, thyme, and sage should keep for up to three weeks stored this way. Remember to change the water every few days.

NUTS AND SEEDS

Nuts and seeds should be stored in a dark, dry, cool place because their oils can go rancid. I keep mine in tightly sealed containers in the freezer. To be sure the nuts and seeds you buy are fresh to begin with, try to buy them in bulk from a store with high turnover, and buy them in quantities that you'll be able to use up within a few months. To really bring out the flavor of nuts, spread them in a single layer on a rimmed baking sheet and toast them in a 350°F oven, tossing once, until fragrant, 8 to 10 minutes. Transfer to a plate to cool. Toast sesame, pumpkin, or sunflower seeds in a small skillet over medium heat, stirring constantly, until they are fragrant and begin to darken, 1 to 3 minutes. Transfer to a plate to cool.

OILS

Make sure you purchase and store your oils in dark glass or opaque bottles or metal cans, since exposure to light will turn oil rancid. You do not have to refrigerate olive or vegetable oils, but they should be kept away from extreme heat. Oils that should be refrigerated include nut and seed oils, which are highly perishable. Most of my recipes call for extra-virgin olive oil, a fruity oil obtained from the first pressing of olives. Among flavorless oils, my favorites are canola, grapeseed, and sunflower. You could also try using pure olive oil, which is much milder than extra-virgin. Oils with a more robust flavor, such as toasted sesame oil should be used sparingly, as a seasoning.

SALT AND PEPPER

These two basic seasonings are indispensable, especially salt. Extremely versatile, salt can balance flavor, tone down acidity, and highlight sweetness. I use coarse sea salt, which contains essential minerals and has a gentle flavor, unlike refined table salt, which is bitter and almost completely lacking in minerals. You can also use kosher salt, which is less expensive. Freshly milled black pepper should be used with a careful hand. Too much can overpower a dish, but too little won't bring out the flavors completely. Since pepper tends to become more concentrated as it cooks, I like to add it when I'm almost done.

SOY SAUCE

Naturally fermented, unpasteurized soy sauces are far more mellow and better tasting than the pasteurized varieties made with refined salt. Natural soy sauce contains beneficial bacteria and aids in digestion. My preferred brand is Nama Shoyu.

SPICES

Buying whole spices and grinding them yourself, as you need them, gives you a much better flavor than preground—and they're less expensive, too! To get the most flavor from whole spices like cumin, caraway, or fennel seeds, toast them in a small skillet over medium-high heat, stirring, until they are fragrant, about 2 minutes. Transfer the seeds to a spice mill or a mortar and grind them to a powder.

SUGAR

Sucanat, made from cane juice, is the most unrefined dry sweetener out there. I call for it in some of the dessert recipes. However, since Sucanat has such a pronounced flavor, there are times when Demerara (raw light brown sugar crystals) or refined white sugar work much better. Sifted organic cane sugar is my choice when a neutral-tasting, refined white sugar is called for. It is milled and washed without the use of bleaches or other chemicals typically used in the refining process. I recommend Florida Crystals, a company whose production is based on the principles of sustainability, such as organic agriculture and renewable energy sources. Their products are available on-line at www.floridacrystals.com and at natural food stores.

VANILLA

The vanilla bean gives a pure flavor and nice black specks but is more expensive and harder to find than vanilla extract. Buy the beans that are full and soft. If you can find only desiccated vanilla beans, soak them in brandy or rum for a few days—they will plump up and the alcohol will become subtly flavored. Pure vanilla extract is alcohol that has been intensely flavored by vanilla beans, and makes a good substitute.

VINEGAR

I like to have on hand red and white wine vinegar, unpasteurized cider vinegar, rice vinegar, sherry vinegar, and a good-quality balsamic vinegar.

WATER

This is the most important ingredient there is. The quality of your water can have a great impact on the food you cook, but most people take it for granted. You shouldn't—either filter it or buy spring water.

EQUIPMENT

Having the right equipment—that is, sturdy, heavy-duty equipment that's made to last—will make cooking easier and faster. Below is a pretty complete list of what you should have in your kitchen to cook most effectively from this book. If you don't have everything on it, don't worry; it can take years to assemble a collection. But here's what to strive for.

BAKING EQUIPMENT

Heavy baking pans—made from black baker's steel, tin, glass, or ceramic—are the best. You should avoid lightweight and nonstick baking pans, which can warp over time.

2 RIMMED BAKING SHEETS (ALSO CALLED JELLY ROLL PANS)

These aluminum pans, usually 11 by 17 inches, are good for toasting nuts and seeds, roasting vegetables, warming bread, and keeping pancakes and *arepas* (South American corn pancakes) warm. You can also flip the pan over and use the underside for baking cookies if you don't have a cookie sheet.

PIE PLATE

I prefer heavy-duty glass or metal pie plates. You can use these to roast fruits and then serve them straight from the pan.

BENRINER

This handy, inexpensive tool (also known as an Asian mandoline) is modeled on the old European cabbage slaw board. It's a flat blade mounted on a slide that allows you to cut vegetables into thin, even slices.

BLENDER

Use blenders for pureeing liquids such as soups and smoothies. If you're shopping for one, I strongly recommend buying an immersion one—a motorized wand used to puree foods right in the bowl or pot. Immersion blenders are easier to use and safer than traditional blenders because you don't need to transfer hot liquids out of the pot and into the blender cup. If you do use a traditional blender to puree hot soups, make sure to fill it only halfway each time to avoid splatter burns.

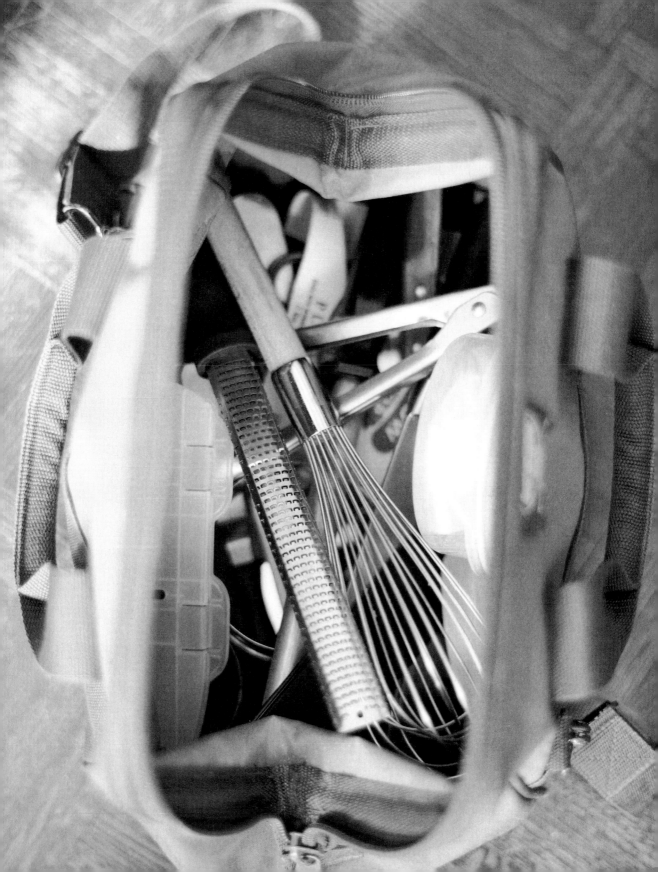

BOWLS

Stainless steel, stackable bowls are lightweight, unbreakable, inexpensive, and don't take up much room. At the very least, you will need three bowls: small (about 6 inches), medium (about 8 inches), and large (about 12 inches). I find that having two medium bowls is helpful. Small, stackable glass bowls are very useful for temporarily storing and then transporting chopped herbs, garlic, onions, and so on. You can also use ramekins or teacups if you like.

BOX GRATER

A four-sided box grater gives you the choice of four different hole sizes and textures for grating cheese and shredding vegetables. Make sure you get a large, sturdy one.

COFFEE MILL (ELECTRIC)

I recommend using a coffee mill for hard-to-grind spices, such as cinnamon sticks, cardamom pods, and whole cloves. For other spices, I prefer using a mortar and pestle.

COLANDER

A 12-inch, stainless steel colander is essential for draining pasta and greens. You can also use the insert from a pasta pot.

CUTTING BOARD

I recommend John Boos cutting boards (available at kitchenware stores), which are made from maple wood. Wooden blocks are the most hygienic because they don't harbor bacteria—there are natural bacteria-killing resins in the wood. Wooden cutting boards also don't dull your knives. Never put them in the dishwasher, and make sure they are thoroughly dried before putting them away. Remember to rub oil on your board every few months to keep it supple (see below).

FOOD PROCESSOR

This is a great tool for quick cooking. Use it to grate cheese, chop or shred vegetables, make dough, and puree foods that aren't too liquidy. Any 8-cup food processor is the perfect size.

KNIVES

For the recipes in this book, you'll need a 2- to 3-inch paring knife, a 6- to 8-inch all-purpose chef's knife, and a bread knife with a serrated edge. I also find a smaller serrated knife handy for cutting citrus.

LADLES

Get a 6- to 8-ounce ladle for soups and stews and a 2- to 4-ounce one for sauces and pancake batter.

MEASURING CUPS AND SPOONS

You need separate sets of dry and wet

CARING FOR YOUR WOODEN TOOLS

To prevent them from drying out and cracking over time, I treat my wooden spoons and cutting boards with food-grade mineral oil once every few months. Use a paper towel to lightly apply the oil, then wipe off the excess. They are now ready to use.

measures, since they are calibrated slightly differently. It's useful to have a 2-cup, 4-cup, and 6-cup measure for liquids. A nesting set of 1 cup, ½ cup, ⅓ cup, and ¼ cup measures is perfect for dry ingredients. I recommend oval-shaped measuring spoons, which, unlike bulky round ones, can fit into small spice jars.

MORTAR AND PESTLE

Vegetarian food gets a lot of its character from ground spices. Purchased, preground spices have a flat flavor, while freshly ground spices are vibrant and have a well-rounded taste. A mortar and pestle are just about as quick as an electric spice grinder, more durable, and much easier to clean. I use a marble mortar with a wooden pestle. A large (6-inch) mortar allows you to crush garlic, spices, and herbs at the same time. You can also make salad dressings right in your mortar, and then use it as an attractive serving vessel.

PEELERS

Get a carbon-steel vegetable peeler, which won't dull over time like stainless steel. I recommend a wide one, rather than a swivel peeler.

PIZZA STONE

A pizza stone will keep your oven at a more even temperature. If you have one, always keep it in the bottom of your oven. If you don't have one, you can use the flip side of your rimmed baking sheet for cooking pizzas.

POTS AND PANS

As a rule, I recommend getting ovenproof pots and pans. They are more durable and you can pop them in the oven to finish cooking, keep warm, or reheat your dish.

SAUCEPANS

Straight-sided one-handled pans are useful for cooking grains, small amounts of soup, sauces, and pasta for two. You will need small (1 ½- to 2-quart) and large (3- to 4-quart) lidded saucepans.

DUTCH OVEN (OR AN OVENPROOF CASSEROLE)

This heavy, ovenproof, cast-iron pot can be transferred from stove top to oven to table. You can buy it with or without an enamel coating. I recommend a 4- to 6-quart size.

4- TO 6-QUART POT

A two-handled, heavy-duty, stainless steel or cast-iron pot is great for stews and soups.

PASTA POT/STOCKPOT

A large (8-quart) pot is very versatile and can be used for steaming greens, cooking pasta, and blanching vegetables. I recommend one made from lightweight stainless steel with a colander insert.

COLLAPSIBLE STEAMER INSERT

Buy the biggest one that will fit in your 4-to 6-quart pot. You can also use a pasta pot colander insert.

PAELLA PAN/BRAZIER

These two-handled, lidded pans are terrific for high-heat roasting. They go from stove top to oven, and keep food hot for a long time. I recommend a 10-inch size.

SKILLETS

Slope-sided pans are good for cooking drier foods and things that need to be flipped, such as frittatas and pancakes. I recommend getting two heavy-duty small (6-inch) skillets and one large (10-inch) skillet.

SAUTÉ PAN

These are straight-sided pans with lids. For these recipes, you will need an ovenproof, 10-inch sauté pan. You may also want a 12-inch sauté pan if you anticipate cooking for a crowd.

RASP

Rasps or microplane-style graters, are useful for tasks like zesting lemons and grating hard cheese, and are easier to use for those tasks than a box grater.

RUBBER SPATULA

I suggest you purchase a versatile flat spatula—and splurge on a medium heat-proof one. You can also get a tiny one (2 by 1 inch) for scraping the last drop from a mustard or jam jar, or from the bowl of your mortar.

SALAD SPINNER

This handy tool for washing greens can double as a salad bowl in a pinch. Get a large one with a pull spring. For advance prep, you can wash and spin your greens, blot and cover with a paper towel, then replace the lid and store in your fridge until the next day. Sometimes I spin twice the amount of lettuce I need, use half right then, and store half for the next day's meal. The basket in a salad spinner can also be used like a colander for washing other vegetables.

SIEVE (STRAINER)

Get a 6-inch and an 8-inch double-meshed sieve.

SPOONS

Wooden spoons are essential—make sure you have at least one with a nice long handle. Never put them, or anything wooden, in the dishwasher. Slotted spoons are great for removing things from liquids, but a metal spider, or Asian wire-mesh skimmer, is the best—its wide surface allows you to retrieve more.

TONGS

In addition to serving pasta and removing cooked foods from pots and pans, a set of heavy, professional, 8- to 10-inch-long, spring-loaded, wooden tongs are also great for retrieving toast from a toaster, and they don't damage food as much as metal ones.

WHISKS

Sturdy whisks are essential for mixing thicker batters and polenta. Smaller ones are useful for emulsifying salad dressings.

PRESSURE COOKERS

The pressure cooker is one of my most valued and versatile cooking tools. It cooks grains and beans very quickly and goes from stove top to oven to table. You can get pressure cookers with two lids: one for pressure and one regular, so the cooker can double as a soup pot. Here are a few words of advice on pressure cookers:

MAKE SURE you keep the gasket clean so that it keeps its tight seal.
DON'T FORGET that you've got it on—don't walk away from it!
IT'S IMPORTANT to get the timing right. Once it has come up to pressure, turn your cooker to low.
NEVER FILL the cooker more than two-thirds of the way, or the release valve will blow.
NEVER OPEN the cooker while it is still under pressure.

YOU CAN RELEASE THE PRESSURE IN ONE OF TWO WAYS:
To release the pressure quickly, turn the cooker off, transfer it to the sink, and run cool water on its sides (if you run water directly at the top, some water may leak into the bowl) until the valve releases. Open slowly.

Or, you can fill the sink with a few inches of cool water and sit the cooker in it until the valve releases. Again, open slowly.

Since you cannot see what's going on inside your pressure cooker, it is easy to overcook things. If you need to check on what's cooking, you can always bring the cooker down from pressure and then repressurize it—no harm done! Or, when you're nearing the end of the cooking time, release the pressure, then return the cooker to the stove top without the cover and simmer until done.

Awakening. . . . New leaves. Spears of wild asparagus pierce softening ground. Shoots and sprouts unwind upward. From deep underground comes the tender first growth of carrots and radishes. The clean flavors of dandelion, cress, and lettuce. Everything is new again. Sweet peas nestle like jewels in pale emerald envelopes. We awake early, eagerness flowing through us like

SPRING

sap. The sour pungency of sorrel and onion grass, snapping the heaviness of winter. Our food steams gently, crisp and light, quickening our tired blood. The earth restores us with sprite tonics: wild ginger, green garlic, peppery mustards, fiddleheads, mint, and chive. Once again the impulse seizes us. We rise from the mire to hurl ourselves into the boundless rush of life.

SPRING MENUS

1. Bibb Lettuce and Radish Salad
   with Crème Fraîche Citronette
   Braised Spring Vegetables with Grits,
   Poached Eggs, and Chives

2. Carrot Mint Salad with Currants
   Charmoula Baked Tempeh with
   Vegetable Couscous

3. Rice, Beans, and Peas
   Garlic Soup with Tortillas, Avocado,
   and Lime

4. Spring Tabbouleh
   Lemon Walnut Hummus with
   Warm Pita

5. Scrambled Eggs with Dandelion
   Greens and Goat Cheese
   Baby Artichokes with Lemon
   Vinaigrette

6. Roasted Asparagus with Garlic
   Buttermilk Strata with Portobello
   Mushrooms and Leeks

7. Spinach Soup with Basmati Rice
and Carrots
Curried Chickpea Pancakes with
Spicy Tahini Sauce

8. White Beans with Mustard Vinaigrette
Spring Borscht with Caraway and Dill

9. Vegetables Aioli
Parmesan Toasts

10. Bruschetta with Broccoli Rabe
and Ricotta
Carrot Leek Soup

11. Orzo with Mustard Greens
Warm Chickpea Salad with Shallots
and Red Wine Vinaigrette

12. Sesame Noodles with Tofu
Steaks and Baby Asian Greens
Pea Shoot and Sprout Salad

MENU 1

-

BIBB LETTUCE AND
RADISH SALAD WITH
CRÈME FRAÎCHE
CITRONETTE

-

BRAISED SPRING
VEGETABLES WITH
GRITS, POACHED
EGGS, AND CHIVES

MARKET LIST

FRESH PRODUCE

1 medium head Bibb
    lettuce, (about
    10 ounces)
8 baby artichokes
½ pound sugar
    snap peas
½ bunch thick asparagus,
    about ½ pound
1 bunch baby white turnips
    (½ pound), or regular
    turnips
2 medium carrots
2 bunches scallions
Chives
1 bunch radishes
Garlic
Mint
1 lemon

DAIRY

Unsalted butter
4 large eggs
Crème fraîche

PANTRY

Extra-virgin olive oil
White wine or rice
    vinegar
All-purpose flour
12 ounces medium corn grits
    (white or yellow)
Coarse sea salt or
    kosher salt
Black peppercorns

EQUIPMENT

Salad spinner
Large saucepan with lid
5-quart Dutch oven or
    3-quart brazier
Medium saucepan
Wire whisk
Slotted spoon
Citrus juicer

MENU 1 GAME PLAN

1. Wash and dry the salad
    greens; chill.
2. Whisk the salad dressing;
    chill.
3. Make the grits and
    braised vegetables
    through step 6.
4. Chop the chives.
5. Toss the salad.
6. Finish the braise and
    poach the eggs.
7. Serve the grits, braise,
    and eggs in wide soup
    plates. Serve the salad on
    the side.

SPEED TIP

Pull the strings from the
sugar snap peas and trim
the asparagus while the
other vegetables simmer.

BIBB LETTUCE AND RADISH SALAD WITH CRÈME FRAÎCHE CITRONETTE

CRÈME FRAÎCHE MAKES THIS DRESSING ULTRA CREAMY, BUT YOU CAN SUBSTITUTE SOUR CREAM OR WHOLE-MILK YOGURT.

YIELD: 4 SERVINGS

For the dressing
½ garlic clove
⅓ cup crème fraîche
1 tablespoon freshly squeezed lemon juice
½ teaspoon coarse sea salt or kosher salt
1 tablespoon extra-virgin olive oil
1 tablespoon chopped fresh chives
Freshly milled black pepper

10 ounces Bibb lettuce leaves, separated
  (about 10 cups)
3 to 4 red radishes, thinly sliced

1. Rub the inside of a salad bowl vigorously with the garlic clove half. Add the crème fraîche, lemon juice, and salt; whisk to combine. Whisk in the olive oil and chives and season with black pepper.

2. Add lettuce and radishes and toss. Serve immediately.

RADISHES are one of the first vegetables to mature in the spring. Their crisp roots are a wonderful food to melt away the fats from rich winter fare. Young and tender radish greens are an excellent source of iron and are a component of traditional spring tonics.

BRAISED SPRING VEGETABLES WITH GRITS, POACHED EGGS, AND CHIVES

BRAISING THE VEGETABLES TAKES SOME TIME, BUT THE GRITS IN THIS RECIPE ARE SUPER QUICK. OR YOU CAN SERVE THE VEGETABLES OVER ANOTHER TYPE OF GRAIN OR PASTA. AND DON'T LIMIT YOURSELF TO MAKING THIS ONLY IN THE SPRING. YOU CAN USE THIS RECIPE YEAR-ROUND, AND SUBSTITUTE OTHER SEASONAL VEGETABLES.

YIELD: 4 SERVINGS

For the grits

1 tablespoon unsalted butter or extra-virgin olive oil

1 teaspoon coarse sea salt or kosher salt

1½ cups medium corn grits (white or yellow)

For the vegetables and poached eggs

2 tablespoons extra-virgin olive oil

2 tablespoons unsalted butter

8 baby artichokes, trimmed and quartered
   (see page 23)

½ pound baby white turnips, halved,
   or regular turnips, peeled and cut into 1-inch chunks

2 medium carrots, peeled and thinly sliced on the bias

2 bunches scallions, trimmed, white and 1 inch of
   green thinly sliced, tops cut into 2-inch lengths

2 garlic cloves, thinly sliced

2 tablespoons chopped fresh mint

2 tablespoons unbleached all-purpose flour

2 teaspoons coarse sea salt or kosher salt

2 tablespoons white wine vinegar or rice vinegar

½ pound sugar snap peas, trimmed and
   strings removed (see page 57)

½ pound asparagus, trimmed and sliced on the bias into 1-inch pieces

Freshly milled black pepper

4 large eggs

2 tablespoons finely chopped chives

1. Preheat the oven to 200°F.

2. To prepare the grits, place a large saucepan with 6 cups of water over high heat. When the water reaches a boil, add the butter, salt, and corn grits. Whisk until the mixture comes to a simmer. Reduce the heat to low and cook, stirring occasionally, until the mixture thickens, about 5 to 7 minutes. Cover the pot and transfer to the warm oven until ready to serve.

3. To prepare the vegetables, in a Dutch oven over high heat, warm the oil and butter until the butter has melted. Add the artichokes, turnips, carrots, and thinly sliced scallions and sauté for 5 minutes, stirring occasionally. Lower the heat if the vegetables begin to brown.

4. Stir in the garlic, mint, and flour and sauté for 1 minute, stirring. Add 2½ cups of water. Raise the heat to high, add the salt, and bring to a boil. Reduce the heat and simmer until the vegetables are tender, about 15 minutes.

5. Meanwhile, prepare a poaching liquid for the eggs. Place a medium saucepan with 2 quarts of water and the vinegar over high heat. When the water reaches a boil, reduce the heat to maintain a steady simmer.

6. Add the scallion greens, peas, and asparagus to the vegetable mixture in the Dutch oven. Raise the heat and simmer until the peas and asparagus are crisp-tender and bright green, about 3 minutes. Season with salt and pepper.

7. Crack an egg into a small bowl and gently add it to the poaching liquid. Immediately repeat with remaining eggs. Cook until the eggs set, about 2 to 3 minutes. Turn off the heat.

8. Spoon some grits into each of 4 deep, wide bowls, and spoon some of the vegetable mixture over the grits. Using a slotted spoon, top each serving with a poached egg. Sprinkle with chives and a twist of black pepper. Serve immediately.

PREPPING ARTICHOKES

If you have tender baby artichokes, prepping them is easy and fast, and you don't have to deal with the immature choke. Simply trim off the top portion of the leaves and the tough bottom of the stem, then peel away the tougher outer leaves. If you are using mature artichokes, you'll need to slice off the top third of the leaves and most of the stem, halve the artichokes, then use a metal spoon to scoop out the hairy choke.

MENU 2

·

CARROT MINT SALAD WITH CURRANTS

·

CHARMOULA BAKED TEMPEH WITH VEGETABLE COUSCOUS

MARKET LIST

FRESH PRODUCE

½ pound asparagus

½ pound sugar snap peas

1 pound carrots

½ pound cremini or white button mushrooms

1 medium red onion

Garlic

Mint

Chives

Cilantro

Olives (optional)

3 lemons

PANTRY

Extra-virgin olive oil

Cumin seeds

Coriander seeds

Cayenne pepper

Sweet paprika

8 ounces couscous

Currants

Coarse sea salt or kosher salt

Black peppercorns

DAIRY AND SOY

2 (8-ounce) packages soy tempeh

EQUIPMENT

Large skillet or sauté pan with lid

Medium saucepan with lid

Small saucepan or kettle

Box grater or food processor with grater disk

Wire whisk

Spice mill

Citrus juicer

MENU 2 GAME PLAN

1. Make the carrot salad; cover and chill.
2. Make charmoula.
3. Cook tempeh.
4. Make the vegetable couscous.
5. Fluff the couscous, top with the tempeh, and serve the carrot salad on the side.
6. A dish of olives would be welcome.

SPEED TIPS

1. Juice the lemons for the carrot salad and charmoula at the same time.
2. String the snap peas and trim the asparagus while the onions and mushrooms sauté.

CARROT MINT SALAD
WITH CURRANTS

CURRANTS ADD A LITTLE SWEETNESS TO THIS SALAD. IF YOU
DON'T HAVE ANY YOU CAN USE CHOPPED RAISINS INSTEAD.
IF YOUR CURRANTS SEEM HARD OR DRIED OUT, PLUMP THEM
IN BOILING WATER FOR A FEW MINUTES BEFORE USING.

YIELD: **4** SERVINGS

2 tablespoons freshly squeezed lemon juice
1 tablespoon extra-virgin olive oil
2 tablespoons chopped fresh mint
1 tablespoon minced fresh chives
Coarse sea salt or kosher salt
1 pound carrots, peeled and coarsely shredded
¼ cup dried currants

In a salad bowl, whisk together the lemon juice, oil, mint, chives, and salt to taste. Add the carrots and currants and toss well.

KEEPING MINT FROM TURNING BLACK

Cut mint, like basil or lettuce, turns black as a result of oxidation. If you're going to eat the mint right away you won't have a problem, but if you want to keep a dish like this salad overnight, you should tear the mint instead of chopping it with a knife. You can also try putting a little olive oil on your knife blade to help prevent oxidation.

CHARMOULA BAKED TEMPEH WITH VEGETABLE COUSCOUS

CHARMOULA IS A CLASSIC, SPICY MOROCCAN MARINADE THAT IS GENERALLY USED FOR FISH. IT ALSO WORKS PARTICULARLY WELL WITH TEMPEH, INFUSING IT WITH AN INTENSE, SUCCULENT FLAVOR. TEMPEH BAKED THIS WAY IS GREAT AS IS, OR CAN BE USED AS THE BASIS FOR AN IMPROMPTU STIR FRY, OR FOR KABOBS ON THE GRILL.

YIELD: 4 SERVINGS

For the tempeh
½ cup extra-virgin olive oil
½ cup chopped fresh cilantro
⅓ cup freshly squeezed lemon juice
4 garlic cloves, roughly chopped
2½ teaspoons coarse sea salt or kosher salt
2 teaspoons sweet paprika
2 teaspoons cumin seeds
1 teaspoon coriander seeds
½ teaspoon cayenne pepper
2 (8 ounce) packages soy tempeh,
     cut into 1-inch squares

For the couscous
2 tablespoons extra-virgin olive oil
1 medium red onion, sliced
½ pound cremini or white button mushrooms,
     trimmed and thickly sliced
½ pound asparagus, trimmed and cut into
     ½-inch lengths
½ pound sugar snap peas, trimmed, strings
     removed, very roughly chopped (see page 57)
1 cup couscous
2 teaspoons coarse sea salt or kosher salt

1. To prepare the charmoula for the tempeh, in a medium bowl, whisk 1 ¼ cups of water with the oil, cilantro, lemon juice, garlic, and salt. In a spice grinder (or mortar), grind the paprika, cumin, coriander, and cayenne. Whisk the ground spices into the olive oil mixture.

2. In a large skillet or sauté pan, arrange the tempeh squares in one layer. Pour the spice mixture over the tempeh. Over high heat, bring the mixture to a simmer. Reduce the heat, cover, and simmer until most, but not all, of the liquid is absorbed, about 15 minutes. If it looks too dry, add a little more water.

3. To prepare the couscous, in a medium saucepan over high heat, warm the oil. Add the onion and sauté for 2 minutes. Add the mushrooms and sauté for 6 minutes, until the mushrooms have given off their liquid and begin to caramelize.

4. Meanwhile, in a small saucepan or kettle over high heat, bring 1 ¼ cups of water to a boil. Pour the boiling water over the mushroom mixture. Stir in the asparagus and peas and return the mixture to a simmer. Stir in the couscous and salt and cover the pot. Turn off the heat and let the couscous steam for 5 to 6 minutes.

5. Fluff the couscous with a fork and divide it among 4 plates. Top with the tempeh and serve.

MENU 3

•

RICE, BEANS, AND PEAS

•

GARLIC SOUP WITH TORTILLAS, AVOCADO, AND LIME

MARKET LIST

FRESH PRODUCE
½ pound English peas, or peas in the pod, or 1 cup preshelled peas
1 large or 2 small ripe avocados
1 jalapeño pepper
1 head broccoli
1 medium carrot
1 medium onion
1 head garlic
Cilantro
2 limes

DAIRY
Unsalted butter
Monterey Jack cheese or sour cream

PANTRY
Neutral oil such as canola, sunflower or grapeseed oil
Extra-virgin olive oil
White or sweet red miso
Cumin seeds
Crushed red pepper flakes
12 ounces Basmati rice
1 (15 ounce) can red kidney beans
6 corn tortillas
Coarse sea salt or kosher salt
Black peppercorns

EQUIPMENT
2 large skillets
2 medium saucepans, one with lid
Sieve
Citrus juicer

MENU 3 GAME PLAN
1. Cook the rice.
2. Start the soup: make the broth and strain it.
3. Fry the tortillas.
4. Finish the soup and keep it warm.
5. Finish the rice with beans and peas.

SPEED TIPS
1. Wrap the separated garlic cloves in a towel or piece of cheesecloth and bash them with a rolling pin or heavy skillet.
2. If you have a mandoline (or Japanese Benriner), use it to slice the carrots and jalapeño pepper while the broth simmers.
3. Slice the tortillas into strips while the oil heats.

RICE, BEANS, AND PEAS

IF YOU WANT TO MAKE THIS DISH AND FRESH PEAS ARE NOT
IN SEASON, SUBSTITUTE FROZEN ONES AND CUT THE
COOKING TIME IN HALF.

YIELD: 4 SERVINGS

1 tablespoon unsalted butter
1½ cups basmati rice
½ teaspoon coarse sea salt or kosher salt,
    plus additional to taste
2 tablespoons extra-virgin olive oil
1 teaspoon cumin seeds
½ teaspoon crushed red pepper flakes
1 medium onion, diced
1 (15-ounce) can red kidney beans
1 cup shelled fresh peas
Coarse sea salt or kosher salt
Freshly milled black pepper
¼ pound Monterey Jack cheese, coarsely
    grated (about 1 cup), or sour cream for
    garnish

1. In a medium saucepan over high heat, bring 2¼ cups of water and the butter to a boil. Stir in the rice and salt and return to a boil. Lower the heat, cover, and let simmer for 18 minutes, until the water is absorbed.

2. Meanwhile, warm the oil in a large skillet over medium heat, add the cumin seeds and red pepper flakes, and cook for 1 minute, until fragrant. Add the onion and a pinch of salt. Raise the heat and sauté until the onion softens, about 3 to 4 minutes.

3. Stir in the beans with their liquid and bring to a boil. Stir in the peas and cook until barely tender, about 1 minute. Stir in the cooked rice and season with salt and pepper. Serve immediately with the grated cheese on top.

GARLIC SOUP WITH TORTILLAS, AVOCADO, AND LIME

THIS SOUP IS TRADITIONALLY MADE WITH CHICKEN STOCK, BUT HERE I USE MISO (FERMENTED SOYBEAN PASTE) TO GIVE IT AN INTENSE FLAVOR. MISO IS LIKE VEGETARIAN BOUILLON. DIFFERENT TYPES OF MISO RANGE IN STRENGTH AND COLOR. LIGHT ONES ARE YOUNG AND MILD, WHILE DARKER MISOS, WHICH HAVE BEEN AGED LONGER, ARE SALTIER, RICHER, AND MORE INTENSE. IN THIS RECIPE I CALL FOR A MELLOW WHITE MISO, WHICH HAS ONLY BEEN AGED FOR ABOUT FOUR MONTHS. YOU CAN SUBSTITUTE A RED MISO (AGED FOR SIX TO EIGHT MONTHS) TO BRING IT UP A NOTCH. ANYTHING DARKER WOULD OVERPOWER THE SOUP.

YIELD: 4 SERVINGS

1 head garlic, cloves separated and smashed

1 small bunch fresh cilantro, stems removed from leaves and reserved for broth, leaves coarsely chopped (about ½ cup chopped leaves)

½ cup neutral oil such as canola, grapeseed, or sunflower

6 fresh corn tortillas, halved and cut into ¼-inch-wide strips

Coarse sea salt or kosher salt

1 large ripe avocado, quartered and sliced

2 limes

2 cups bite-size broccoli florettes

1 medium carrot, peeled, halved lengthwise, and sliced thin on the bias

1 jalapeño pepper (with its seeds), sliced into paper-thin rings

½ cup white miso, or to taste

1. To prepare the broth, in a medium saucepan over high heat, combine 6 cups of water, garlic, and the cilantro stems and bring to a boil. Reduce the heat and simmer for 10 minutes. Strain out the solids and return the broth to the saucepan. Cover to keep warm.

2. Heat the oil in a large skillet over medium-high heat until you see the first whisp of smoke. Add the tortilla strips and fry until crisp, about 5 minutes. Remove the tortilla strips, drain on paper towels, and season lightly with salt.

3. Juice 1 lime and cut the other into wedges.

4. In a small bowl, toss the avocado pieces with the lime juice and set aside.

5. Add the broccoli, carrot, and jalapeño to the broth and simmer over medium heat for 2 to 3 minutes, until the vegetables are crisp-tender.

6. Place ½ cup of miso in a small bowl. Add a little of the hot soup broth and stir with a spoon until the miso becomes creamy. Transfer the miso to the soup and simmer for 1 minute. If desired, add more miso to taste. Stir in the chopped cilantro leaves.

7. Divide the tortilla strips and avocado among 4 soup bowls. Ladle the soup into the bowls and serve immediately, accompanied by the lime wedges.

SLICING AVOCADOS

Everyone has their own way of slicing avocados. I prefer to score the avocado lengthwise into quarters, all the way to the pit, so that the peel comes off in four strips. Then you can insert your knife and release the flesh from the pit. You can also cut the avocado in half before peeling it, and twist the halves to separate them and dislodge the pit. Then you take each half in the cup of your hand, slice the flesh with a knife, and pop out the slices out from the skin.

MENU 4

·

SPRING TABBOULEH

·

LEMON WALNUT HUMMUS
WITH WARM PITA

MARKET LIST

FRESH PRODUCE
1 pint cherry tomatoes
1 bunch radishes
Chives
Garlic
2 bunches flat-leaf
    parsley
2 large bunches mint
2 lemons

PANTRY
Extra-virgin olive oil
Cumin seeds
Coriander seeds
Cayenne pepper
8 ounces medium or fine
    bulgur wheat
1 (15-ounce) can
    chickpeas
8 ounces shelled walnuts
Coarse sea salt or
    kosher salt
Olives
Black peppercorns
1 package whole wheat
    pita bread

EQUIPMENT
Small skillet
Medium saucepan with lid
Food processor
Spice mill or mortar and
    pestle
Sieve
Citrus juicer

MENU 4 GAME PLAN
1. Preheat the oven to
   350°F.
2. Make the tabbouleh
   through step 1.
3. Prepare the hummus.
4. Transfer the hummus to a
   bowl, drizzle it with olive
   oil, and sprinkle with
   paprika. Garnish with
   olives.
5. Wrap the pita and warm
   it in the oven.
6. Finish the tabbouleh
   and transfer it to a
   serving bowl.

SPRING TABBOULEH

BULGUR IS A PARCHED GRAIN, MADE FROM WHEAT BERRIES
THAT HAVE BEEN STEAMED, DRIED, AND CRACKED. LIKE ALL
PARTIALLY COOKED GRAINS, BULGUR IS VERY CONVENIENT
BECAUSE IT COOKS FAST. THIS EFFICIENCY IS ONE OF THE
REASONS THAT BULGUR AND OTHER PARCHED GRAINS ARE
COMMONLY USED IN PLACES WHERE FUEL IS SCARCE.
DIFFERENT TYPES OF BULGUR COME FROM DIFFERENT TYPES
OF WHEAT. IF YOU HAVE A CHOICE, THE ONE I RECOMMEND
IS MADE FROM GOLDEN DURUM WHEAT, WHICH PRODUCES A
LIGHTER TASTE AND BETTER COLOR THAN BULGUR MADE
FROM DARKER VARIETIES OF WINTER WHEAT. THERE ARE
ALSO DIFFERENT GRADES, RANGING FROM FINE TO
COARSE—I PREFER A MEDIUM GRADE.

YIELD: **4** SERVINGS

½ teaspoon coarse sea salt or
   kosher salt, plus additional to taste
1 cup medium or fine bulgur wheat
2 cups chopped fresh mint leaves
1 cup chopped fresh flat-leaf parsley
¼ cup finely chopped fresh chives
4 or 5 radishes, thinly sliced
2 tablespoons freshly squeezed lemon juice
2 tablespoons extra-virgin olive oil
Freshly milled black pepper
1 cup cherry tomatoes, halved

1. In a medium saucepan over high heat, bring 1 ¼ cups of
water and the ½ teaspoon of salt to a boil. Stir in the bulgur
and simmer, covered, for 30 seconds. Remove the pan from
the heat and set aside for 20 minutes. Transfer the bulgur to
a serving bowl, fluff with a fork, and let cool.

2. When the bulgur has cooled, stir in the mint, parsley,
chives, and radishes. Add the lemon juice and oil and stir to
combine. Season with salt and pepper. Gently stir in the
tomatoes and serve.

PITA BREAD

Here is a simple way to make everyday, store-bought whole wheat or white pita special: Lightly moisten a clean cotton towel. Wrap the pita in the towel and place in a 350°F oven for 10 to 15 minutes.

LEMON WALNUT HUMMUS
WITH WARM PITA

MOST HUMMUS IS MADE WITH TAHINI (SESAME PASTE), BUT
THIS ONE IS BASED ON WALNUTS, WHICH GIVE IT A UNIQUE,
TOASTED FLAVOR. HUMMUS IS READILY AVAILABLE IN
SUPERMARKETS NOW, BUT COMMERCIAL BRANDS JUST
DON'T COMPARE WITH HOMEMADE, WHICH ISN'T ALL THAT
DIFFICULT TO MAKE.

YIELD: 2 CUPS

½ cup walnuts, coarsely chopped
1 teaspoon cumin seeds
½ teaspoon coriander seeds
¼ teaspoon cayenne pepper
1 (15-ounce) can chickpeas, drained
¼ cup extra-virgin olive oil
3 tablespoons freshly squeezed lemon juice
2 garlic cloves, coarsely chopped
1 teaspoon coarse sea salt or
    kosher salt, plus additional to taste
Olives for serving
1 package whole wheat pita bread
    (see page 33)

1. Preheat the oven to 350°F.

2. In a small skillet over medium heat, toast the walnuts for 2 to 3 minutes, shaking the pan occasionally to ensure even browning. Transfer the nuts to a sieve to cool.

3. Add the cumin and coriander seeds to the skillet and toast for 30 seconds. Transfer to a spice mill or mortar and pestle, add the cayenne pepper, and grind to a powder.

4. In a food processor, combine the chickpeas, oil, lemon juice, garlic, ground spices, and 1 teaspoon of the salt.

5. Rub the walnuts against a sieve over the sink to remove most of their papery skins. Add the skinned walnuts to the processor, and puree until smooth. Add water, 1 tablespoon at a time, if the hummus is thicker than you like. Season with additional salt, garnish with olives, and serve with pita bread.

MENU 5

•

SCRAMBLED EGGS WITH DANDELION GREENS AND GOAT CHEESE

•

BABY ARTICHOKES WITH LEMON VINAIGRETTE

MARKET LIST

FRESH PRODUCE

1 pound dandelion greens

12 baby artichokes

Radish sprouts or parsley

1 medium onion

Garlic

Thyme

2 lemons

DAIRY

8 large eggs

8 ounces fresh goat cheese

PANTRY

Extra-virgin olive oil

Crushed red pepper flakes

Coarse sea salt or kosher salt

Black peppercorns

Country-style bread

EQUIPMENT

Large pot

Large skillet or sauté pan

Large pressure cooker

Citrus juicer

Salad spinner

MENU 5 GAME PLAN

1. Fill a large pot with water and place over high heat.
2. Make the artichokes through step 2.
3. Make the eggs.
4. Finish the artichokes.
5. Serve the eggs with artichokes on the side, accompanied with a good loaf of bread.

SPEED TIP

Wash the dandelion greens in a salad spinner filled with cold water, drain, and spin dry.

SCRAMBLED EGGS WITH DANDELION GREENS AND GOAT CHEESE

TAKE CARE NOT TO OVERSCRAMBLE YOUR EGGS. IF YOU TURN OFF THE HEAT JUST BEFORE THEY ARE DONE, WHEN THEY ARE STILL A LITTLE RUNNY, THEY'LL FINISH UP IN THE PAN AND BECOME CREAMY AND FLUFFY. YOU CAN SUBSTITUTE OTHER TENDER GREENS, LIKE CHARD, MUSTARD OR SPINACH, FOR THE DANDELION.

YIELD: 4 SERVINGS

1 pound dandelion greens,
    ends trimmed
8 large eggs
½ pound fresh goat cheese,
    crumbled
¼ teaspoon coarse sea salt or kosher salt
¼ cup extra-virgin olive oil
1 medium onion, thinly sliced
⅛ teaspoon crushed red pepper flakes

1. Fill a large pasta pot three-quarters full with water and bring to a boil. Add the dandelion greens and return to a boil. Boil the greens until they are tender, 2 to 3 minutes. Drain well.

2. In a large bowl, whisk together the eggs, goat cheese, and salt.

3. In a large skillet over medium-high heat, warm the oil. Add the onion and red pepper flakes and sauté until the onion is browned around the edges, about 3 minutes.

4. Gently squeeze the blanched greens to remove any excess water. Roughly chop the greens, add them to the skillet with the onions, and sauté for 1 minute. Add the egg mixture to the pan and scramble over medium heat until done to your taste. Serve immediately.

BABY ARTICHOKES WITH LEMON VINAIGRETTE

HERE'S ANOTHER GREAT USE FOR YOUR PRESSURE COOKER—YOU'VE NEVER SEEN ARTICHOKES COOK THIS FAST! IF YOU DO NOT HAVE A PRESSURE COOKER, SIMMER THE ARTICHOKES IN 1 ⅔ CUPS OF WATER FOR 18 TO 20 MINUTES UNTIL TENDER.

YIELD: 4 SERVINGS

¼ cup extra-virgin olive oil, plus
   additional for serving
¼ cup freshly squeezed lemon juice
4 garlic cloves, halved lengthwise
3 sprigs fresh thyme
1 teaspoon coarse sea salt or
   kosher salt, plus additional to taste
½ teaspoon black peppercorns
12 baby artichokes, trimmed and
   halved lengthwise (see page 23)
Radish sprouts or chopped parsley

1. Combine ⅔ cup water, the oil, lemon juice, garlic, thyme, salt, and the peppercorns in a pressure cooker.

2. Add the artichokes to the pressure cooker and lock the lid in place. Bring to full pressure over high heat. Reduce the heat to low and cook for 2 minutes.

3. Transfer the pot to the sink and run cold water over it to release the pressure.

4. Transfer the artichokes in their juices to a bowl and drizzle with olive oil, season with salt, and garnish with the radish sprouts or chopped parsley.

MENU 6

•

ROASTED ASPARAGUS
WITH GARLIC

•

BUTTERMILK STRATA
WITH PORTOBELLO
MUSHROOMS AND LEEKS

MARKET LIST

FRESH PRODUCE

2 bunches thick
    asparagus
1 pound portobello
    mushrooms
2 medium leeks
Garlic
Flat-leaf parsley
Thyme
1 lemon

DAIRY

2 cups buttermilk
6 large eggs
4 ounces fresh whole-milk
    ricotta cheese
4 ounces Parmesan or
    Grana Padano cheese

PANTRY

Extra-virgin olive oil
Dry white wine
½ pound day old country-
    style artisanal bread
Black peppercorns
Coarse sea salt or
    kosher salt

EQUIPMENT

10-inch oven proof sauté
    pan
Rimmed baking sheet
    (11 x 17 inches)
Box grater

MENU 6 GAME PLAN

1. Preheat the oven.
2. Prepare the strata.
3. Roast the asparagus.
4. Slice the lemon.
5. Serve the strata,
   accompanied by the
   asparagus and lemon
   wedges.

ROASTED ASPARAGUS
WITH GARLIC

ROASTED ASPARAGUS HAS A NUTTIER, RICHER FLAVOR THAN
ITS STEAMED COUNTERPART.

YIELD: **4** SERVINGS

2 bunches thick asparagus,
    trimmed
¼ cup extra-virgin olive oil
4 garlic cloves, finely chopped
1 teaspoon coarse sea salt or
    kosher salt
Freshly milled black pepper
Lemon wedges for serving

1. Preheat the oven to 450°F.

2. Arrange the asparagus on a rimmed baking sheet in a single layer. Sprinkle with the oil, garlic, salt, and pepper and roll them to coat.

3. Roast in the oven until crisp-tender, about 8 to 10 minutes.

4. Serve with lemon wedges.

**GILDING THE LILY:
MAKING BROTH FROM
TRIMMINGS**

Mushroom stems, leek greens, and asparagus ends should really be saved for broth rather than discarded. To make a broth, simply toss the clean trimmings along with some herbs of your choice in a pot with water to cover, and simmer for 20 minutes. Strain the broth and add salt to taste. The broth is excellent for soup, stew, or risotto. It will keep for 3 days if refrigerated and up to 3 months if frozen. If you don't have time to make the broth right away, just put the trimmings in a plastic bag and store in the fridge for up to 5 days.

BUTTERMILK STRATA WITH PORTOBELLO MUSHROOMS AND LEEKS

STRATAS ARE GREAT FOR USING UP DAY-OLD ARTISANAL BREAD, WHICH I THINK IS TOO TASTY TO THROW OUT!

YIELD: 4 TO 6 SERVINGS

6 large eggs

2 cups buttermilk

¼ pound fresh whole-milk ricotta cheese

½ cup finely chopped fresh flat-leaf parsley

2 medium leeks, white and tender green
    parts only, cleaned (see page 61), thinly sliced

3 tablespoons extra-virgin olive oil

2 garlic cloves, roughly chopped

1 tablespoon fresh thyme leaves, minced

2 teaspoons coarse sea salt or kosher salt

½ teaspoon freshly milled black pepper

1 pound portobello mushrooms, stems removed,
    and caps diced

½ cup dry white wine

½ pound day-old, country-style artisanal bread,
    cut into 1-inch cubes

¼ cup freshly grated Parmesan or Grana Padano cheese

1. Set a rack on the middle shelf of the oven and preheat to 450°F.

2. In a medium bowl, whisk the eggs, buttermilk, ricotta cheese, and parsley, and set aside.

3. Place a 10-inch sauté pan or brazier over high heat. When the pan is hot, add the leeks and cook until lightly browned, about 2 minutes.

4. Keep the heat high and add the oil, garlic, thyme, salt, and pepper and sauté, stirring, for 1 minute.

5. Add the mushrooms and wine and bring to a simmer. Stir in the bread cubes.

6. Pour the egg mixture over all and stir to combine.

7. Sprinkle the grated cheese over the top. Place the pan in the oven and bake until the strata has set, about 25 minutes.

MENU 7

•

SPINACH SOUP
WITH BASMATI RICE
AND CARROTS

•

CURRIED CHICKPEA
PANCAKES WITH SPICY
TAHINI SAUCE

MARKET LIST

FRESH PRODUCE

1 (10-ounce) bag
   prewashed baby spinach
   or 1 large bunch spinach
   (about ¾ pound)
4 medium carrots
1 bunch scallions
1 medium onion
Garlic
Dill
Cilantro
1 lemon

DAIRY

4 large eggs
8 ounces plain yogurt
   (whole or low-fat)

PANTRY

Extra-virgin olive oil
Neutral oil such as
   grapeseed, canola oil, or
   sunflower oil
Cumin seeds or ground
   cumin
Curry powder
Cayenne pepper
4 ounces basmati rice
8 ounces unbleached
   all-purpose flour
1 pound chickpea flour
Baking powder
Tahini
Coarse sea salt or
   kosher salt
Black peppercorns

EQUIPMENT

1 or 2 small nonstick skillets
Large saucepan with lid
Rimmed baking sheet
   (11 x 17 inches)
Blender or food processor
Whisk
Spice mill
Citrus juicer

MENU 7 GAME PLAN

1. Preheat the oven and make
   the soup through step 4.
2. Rinse and chop the dill.
3. Prepare the tahini sauce;
   cover and set aside.
4. Make the pancakes
   through step 2.
5. Stir the dill into the soup
   and simmer until done.
6. Finish the pancakes.
7. Serve the pancakes
   drizzled with sauce and
   garnished with cilantro.
   Accompany with the
   soup.

SPINACH SOUP WITH BASMATI RICE AND CARROTS

I RECOMMEND BUYING BAGS OF ORGANIC, PREWASHED BABY SPINACH—IT'S REALLY A BIG TIME-SAVER. IF YOU DO BUY BUNCHES OF SPINACH, MAKE SURE TO REMOVE ANY TOUGH STEMS AND WASH THEM THOROUGHLY TO REMOVE ALL THE GRIT.

YIELD: 4 SERVINGS

3 tablespoons extra-virgin olive oil
1 medium onion, diced
1 (10-ounce) bag prewashed baby spinach
    or 1 large bunch spinach (about ¾ pound),
    trimmed and washed
4 medium carrots, peeled and cut
    into thin coins
⅓ cup basmati rice
3 garlic cloves, minced
1 teaspoon cumin seeds, toasted and ground
    (see page 8), or 1 teaspoon ground cumin
1 teaspoon coarse sea salt or kosher salt,
    plus additional to taste
¼ cup chopped fresh dill
2 tablespoons freshly squeezed lemon juice
Freshly milled black pepper

1. In a large saucepan over medium heat, warm the olive oil. Add the onions and cook, stirring occasionally, until tender, about 5 minutes.

2. Meanwhile, in a blender or food processor, working in batches, puree the spinach with 1 cup of water until smooth.

3. Add the carrots, rice, garlic, and cumin to the onions and cook, stirring, for 1 minute.

4. Add the spinach puree, 3 cups of water, and salt and bring to a boil. Reduce the heat and simmer, covered, for 15 minutes, stirring occasionally.

5. Stir in the dill and simmer, covered, until the rice is tender, 3 to 4 minutes. Add the lemon juice and season with salt and pepper. Add additional water if the soup is too thick.

CURRIED CHICKPEA PANCAKES WITH SPICY TAHINI SAUCE

I SERVE THESE PANCAKES SILVER DOLLAR SIZE FOR COCKTAIL PARTIES WITH EITHER SPICY TAHINI SAUCE (SEE PAGE 47) OR YOGURT SAUCE (SEE PAGE 258). YOU CAN DOUBLE THE TAHINI SAUCE RECIPE AND USE IT LATER FOR IMPROMPTU CRUDITÉS SNACKING. IT WILL KEEP FOR A WEEK, COVERED, IN THE FRIDGE.

YIELD: 4 SERVINGS

2 cups chickpea flour

1 cup unbleached all-purpose flour

2 teaspoons baking powder

2 tablespoons curry powder

1 tablespoon coarse sea salt or
    kosher salt

Freshly milled black pepper

1 cup plain yogurt

4 large eggs, lightly beaten

3 tablespoons neutral oil, such as
    grapeseed, canola, or sunflower

6 scallions, trimmed and thinly sliced

1 cup chopped fresh cilantro, plus additional
    sprigs for garnish

Tahini Sauce (recipe follows)

1. Place a heavy rimmed baking sheet in the oven and preheat to 200°F.

2. In a large bowl, whisk together the chickpea flour, all-purpose flour, baking powder, curry powder, salt, and pepper. In a medium bowl, whisk together 2 cups of water, the yogurt, eggs, and 2 tablespoons of the oil. Pour the wet mixture over the dry mixture and stir to combine. Add the scallions and chopped cilantro and mix well.

3. Place one or two small, nonstick skillets over medium heat. Coat with the remaining 1 tablespoon of oil and heat for 30 seconds. Ladle ⅔ cup of batter into the pan(s). Fry for 4 minutes until the surface of the pancake has begun to dry out and the underside is golden brown. Flip and fry for 3 minutes more. Transfer the cooked pancakes to the heated baking pan and keep warm in the oven. Repeat until the batter is used up.

4. Transfer the cooked pancakes to a clean cutting board and cut each one into 4 wedges.

5. To serve, arrange 4 to 6 wedges on each of 4 plates. Spoon tahini sauce on top and garnish with cilantro sprigs.

TAHINI SAUCE

¾ cup tahini
¾ cup water
¼ cup plus 1 tablespoon freshly squeezed lemon juice
1 garlic clove, minced
¾ teaspoon coarse sea salt or kosher salt
¼ teaspoon cayenne pepper

In a small bowl, combine all ingredients and whisk until smooth.

YIELD: ABOUT 1¾ CUPS

MENU 8

•

WHITE BEANS WITH MUSTARD VINAIGRETTE

•

SPRING BORSCHT WITH CARAWAY AND DILL

MARKET LIST

FRESH PRODUCE
1 bunch beet greens or
    Swiss chard
Celery
2 medium golden or
    red beets
1 large or 2 medium
    carrots
1 bunch parsley or chives
1 large onion
1 small red onion
Garlic
Dill

DAIRY
Unsalted butter (if not
    using oil)

PANTRY
Extra-virgin olive oil
    (if not using butter)
Apple cider vinegar
Red wine vinegar
Dijon-style mustard
Caraway seeds
Sugar, maple syrup, or
    honey
2 (15-ounce) cans navy
    beans
Coarse sea salt or
    kosher salt
Black peppercorns
1 loaf artisanal bread

EQUIPMENT
Large saucepan with lid
Medium saucepan
Box grater or food processor
Sieve
Spice grinder

MENU 8 GAME PLAN
1. Make the soup through
   step 2.
2. Make the beans through
   step 2.
3. Prep the soup greens.
4. Finish the soup.
5. Finish the white beans.
6. Serve the soup and white
   beans, accompanied by
   good bread.

WHITE BEANS WITH MUSTARD VINAIGRETTE

IF YOU ARE REALLY PRESSED FOR TIME, SKIP THE
BLANCHING STEP FOR THE ONION AND CELERY. THE
SALAD WON'T BE AS REFINED, BUT WILL HAVE A
NICE, FIRM CRUNCH.

YIELD: **4** TO **6** SERVINGS

3 tablespoons red wine vinegar
2 tablespoons Dijon-style mustard
1 tablespoon coarse sea salt or
    kosher salt, plus additional to taste
4 tablespoons extra-virgin olive oil
1 cup finely diced celery
¼ cup finely diced red onion
2 (15-ounce) cans navy beans, drained
    and rinsed
Freshly milled black pepper
Chopped fresh parsley or chives for
    garnish

1. In a large bowl, whisk together the vinegar, mustard, and 1 teaspoon of the salt. Whisk in the oil.

2. In a medium saucepan over high heat, bring 6 cups of water to a boil. Add the remaining 2 teaspoons of salt. When the water returns to a boil, add the celery and onion and blanch for 1 minute. Drain well and toss with the vinaigrette.

3. Add the beans to the vinaigrette. Mix well and season with salt and pepper. Sprinkle with parsley or chives and serve.

SPRING BORSCHT WITH CARAWAY AND DILL

YOUR FOOD PROCESSOR'S GRATER ATTACHMENT WILL CUT
WAY DOWN ON PREP TIME FOR THIS SOUP, BUT YOU CAN
ALSO USE A BOX GRATER. KEEP IN MIND THAT THE SUGAR IN
THE SOUP IS OPTIONAL. YOU MAY WISH TO ADD MORE OR
LESS, DEPENDING ON THE NATURAL SWEETNESS OF THE
BEETS. YOU CAN ALSO SUBSTITUTE HONEY OR MAPLE SYRUP
IF YOU PREFER. I FIND THAT SOME ADDED SWEETNESS
WORKS WELL WITH THE TANGY VINEGAR TO CREATE A
ROUND, ENHANCED FLAVOR, WHICH MAKES THIS
DECEPTIVELY SIMPLE SOUP SEEM MORE COMPLEX. FOR A
SLIGHTLY BRIGHTER-HUED SOUP, YOU CAN PEEL THE
CARROTS AND BEETS, BUT I DON'T FIND THIS NECESSARY.

YIELD: **4** SERVINGS

2 tablespoons extra-virgin olive oil or
   unsalted butter
1 large onion, halved and thinly sliced
Coarse sea salt or kosher salt
1 garlic clove, finely chopped
1 teaspoon caraway seeds, toasted and
   ground (see page 8)
2 medium golden or red beets, coarsely
   grated
1 large or 2 medium carrots, coarsely
   grated
2 cups firmly packed thinly sliced
   beet greens or Swiss chard
2 tablespoons apple cider vinegar,
   or to taste
2 teaspoons sugar, preferably organic
   washed cane sugar (see page 8),
   or maple syrup, or honey, or to taste
1 tablespoon finely chopped fresh dill
Freshly milled black pepper

1. In a large saucepan over medium heat, warm the oil or melt the butter. Add the onion and sauté with a pinch of salt until softened, about 5 minutes. Stir in the garlic and caraway and sauté for 2 minutes. Add the beets and carrot, cover with 3 cups of water, and bring to a boil. Reduce the heat and simmer, covered, until the vegetables are tender, about 15 to 20 minutes.

2. Add the beet greens, vinegar, and sugar and simmer until the greens are tender, about 3 to 5 minutes. Stir in the dill. Season with salt and pepper and additional sugar or honey if desired. Serve immediately.

MENU 9

•

VEGETABLES AIOLI

•

PARMESAN TOASTS

MARKET LIST

FRESH PRODUCE

1 lemon

Garlic

1 package hearts of romaine

½ pound sugar snap peas

1 bunch asparagus

2 fennel bulbs

Celery

1 head broccoli

1 head cauliflower

1 bunch beets

3 to 4 carrots

DAIRY

1 large egg

4 to 6 ounces Parmesan cheese

PANTRY

Neutral oil such as grapeseed,
    canola, or sunflower

Extra-virgin olive oil

Dijon Mustard

Coarse sea salt or
    kosher salt

Black peppercorns

1 loaf country bread

1 bottle crisp white wine

EQUIPMENT

Large stockpot

Small saucepan

Pressure cooker

Rimmed baking sheet

Box grater

Garlic press

Wire whisk

Pastry brush

MENU 9 GAME PLAN

1. Preheat the oven to 375°F.
   Survey your haul of
   vegetables. Decide what
   you would like to serve
   cooked and what appeals
   to you raw.

2. Bring a large pot of water
   to a boil.

3. Prepare the aioli, cover,
   and set aside.

4. Prep the vegetables.

5. Salt the boiling water.

6. Blanch the vegetables and
   arrange artfully on platters.

7. Make the Parmesan toasts.

8. Open a crisp bottle of white
   wine and enjoy dinner.

SPEED TIPS

1. Aioli can be made in a food
   processor if the plunger for
   the feed tube has a tiny
   hole in it, through which
   the olive oil will drip in
   slowly (many do, expressly
   for this purpose).

2. For an aioli with a more
   pronounced garlic flavor,
   which many people
   prefer, skip the blanching
   step. Just make sure your
   garlic is very fresh and
   remove the green germ
   from each clove.

VEGETABLES AIOLI

IF YOU'VE EVER BEEN TO A FARMER'S MARKET, YOU KNOW
HOW HARD IT CAN BE TO RESIST THE IMPULSE TO GO WILD
RAIDING THE INEVITABLE BOUNTY OF TEMPTING FRESH
PRODUCE PILED HIGH ON THE VENDORS' TABLES. HERE IS MY
SOLUTION FOR AN EVENING MEAL ON SUCH AN OCCASION: A
MIXTURE OF RAW AND LIGHTLY COOKED VEGETABLES WORKS
BEST. YOU CAN ALSO ADD COOKED CHICKPEAS, STEAMED
TOFU, AND HARD-BOILED EGGS FOR A HEARTIER MEAL.
FOR A COLORFUL, MEDLEY WITH GOOD TEXTURE, I
RECOMMEND COOKED PEELED BEETS, BLANCHED BROCCOLI
AND CAULIFLOWER FLORETS, BLANCHED ASPARAGUS, BLANCHED
SUGAR SNAP PEAS, RAW FENNEL, AND RAW CARROT AND CELERY
STICKS. OR USE ANY COMBINATION OF SEASONAL VEGETABLES.

YIELD: **4 SERVINGS**

1 head broccoli, separated into florets
1 head cauliflower, separated into florets
1 bunch asparagus, trimmed and blanched
½ pound sugar snap peas, trimmed (see page 57)
1 bunch beets, trimmed
2 fennel bulbs, trimmed and cut lengthwise into eighths
3 to 4 carrots, peeled and cut into sticks
½ bunch head celery, cut into sticks
Hearts of romaine, separated into leaves
Aioli (recipe follows)

1. Bring a large pot of water to a boil. Add salt and then, one vegetable at a time, blanch the broccoli, cauliflower, asparagus, and sugar snap peas, or seasonal vegetables of your choice, until tender, about 2 to 4 minutes, depending upon the vegetable. Remove each vegetable as it is done with a slotted spoon and return the water to a boil before adding the next one.

2. Put the beets in a pressure cooker over high heat, with water to cover. Lock the lid in place and cook at full pressure, about 8 minutes for large beets and 6 minutes for small ones. Transfer the pot to sink and run cold water over it to bring down the pressure. Cool the beets under cold running water and slip off their skins. Slice the beets into wedges before serving.

3. Serve the vegetables on a large platter accompanied by the aioli, coarse sea salt or kosher salt, lemon wedges, and the Parmesan toasts.

AIOLI

TO MAKE A GOOD AIOLI, IT'S CRUCIAL TO USE EGG YOLKS THAT ARE AT ROOM TEMPERATURE AND TO ADD THE OIL IN A SLOW DRIZZLE. WHEN I MAKE MY AIOLI, I COMBINE THE OILS IN A NARROW-NECK BOTTLE SO I CAN COVER THE OPENING WITH MY THUMB. IT ALLOWS ME TO ADD THE OIL DROP BY DROP. YOU CAN ALSO USE A FOOD PROCESSOR AND GRADUALLY POUR IN THE OILS IN A STEADY STREAM WHILE THE PROCESSOR IS ON.

YIELD: **4** SERVINGS

½ cup neutral oil, such as canola,
   grapeseed, or sunflower
½ cup extra-virgin olive oil
4 garlic cloves, peeled and left whole
1 large egg yolk at room temperature
1 teaspoon Dijon-style mustard
½ teaspoon coarse sea salt or kosher
   salt, or to taste
2 tablespoons freshly squeezed lemon juice
Freshly milled black pepper

1. In a bottle with an opening small enough so that your thumb will cover it (such as a wine or beer bottle) shake together the canola and olive oils to mix. Anchor a heavy mixing bowl to the counter by placing it on top of a slightly damp, coiled kitchen towel.

2. In a small saucepan over high heat, bring 2 cups of water to a boil. Add the garlic cloves and simmer for 5 minutes. Drain and cool under cold running water. Using a garlic press, crush the garlic into the mixing bowl. Add the egg yolk, mustard, and salt, and whisk until smooth.

3. With one hand dribble the oils drop by drop into the egg mixture while whisking constantly with the other hand. Continue in this way until the egg starts to thicken. Gradually increase the flow of oil until it has been completely incorporated. You will have a thick, glossy mayonnaise. Whisk in the lemon juice. Whisk in a little water, 1 tablespoon at a time, until you create a thick, pourable sauce. Season with salt and pepper.

PARMESAN TOASTS

HERE IS A SIMPLE AND SAVORY WAY TO VAMP UP
THE CRUNCH OF TOASTED ARTISANAL BREAD.

YIELD: **4** SERVINGS

1 loaf country bread, sliced
   ½ inch thick
Extra-virgin olive oil for brushing
Freshly milled black pepper
½ cup grated Parmesan cheese

1. Set one rack on the top shelf and one rack on the middle shelf of the oven and preheat to 375°F.

2. Arrange the bread slices on a rimmed baking sheet. Brush liberally with olive oil and season with pepper. Toast on the middle shelf of the oven for 10 minutes.

3. Remove the toasted slices from the oven and sprinkle the cheese over the slices. Return the slices to the oven, this time placing the baking sheet on the top rack, and toast until the cheese is golden brown, about 5 minutes. Serve immediately.

PREPPING SNAP PEAS

Snap peas are great because you do not need to shell them; the pods are tender and juicy. However, there are two strings on the top and bottom of the pea that should be removed. Just snap the stem and pull both strings off at once.

MENU 10

•

**BRUSCHETTA WITH
BROCCOLI RABE AND
RICOTTA**

•

CARROT LEEK SOUP

MARKET LIST

FRESH PRODUCE

1 ½ pounds broccoli rabe

2 pounds baby carrots

2 medium leeks

Garlic

Tarragon

1 orange

DAIRY

Unsalted butter

12 ounces fresh ricotta

Pecorino cheese

PANTRY

Extra-virgin olive oil

Maple syrup or honey

Crushed red pepper
   flakes

Golden raisins

Coarse sea salt or
   kosher salt

Black peppercorns

1 loaf country bread

EQUIPMENT

Large pot

Large skillet or sauté pan

Pressure cooker

Blender or food
   processor

Box grater

Citrus juicer

MENU 10 GAME PLAN

1. Bring a large pot of water
   to a boil.
2. Preheat the oven to
   500°F.
3. Make the soup through
   step 2.
4. Prepare the bruschetta.
5. Finish the soup and serve,
   accompanied by
   bruschetta.

SPEED TIP

If you have an immersion
blender, it makes pureeing
soup much faster.

BRUSCHETTA WITH BROCCOLI RABE AND RICOTTA

BRUSCHETTA IS TYPICALLY THOUGHT OF AS GARLICKY TOAST
TOPPED WITH FRESH CHOPPED TOMATOES AND BASIL. HERE,
WE'RE MAKING A MAIN COURSE OPEN-FACED SANDWICH
WITH BROCCOLI RABE AND SWEET, MILKY RICOTTA. FRESH
RICOTTA WILL MAKE ALL THE DIFFERENCE HERE.

YIELD: 4 SERVINGS

1½ pounds broccoli rabe, trimmed
    and cut into 1-inch lengths
¼ cup extra-virgin olive oil
4 garlic cloves, thinly sliced
½ cup golden raisins
¼ teaspoon crushed red pepper
    flakes
Coarse sea salt or kosher salt
4 thick slices country bread
1⅓ cups fresh ricotta cheese
Grated pecorino cheese for garnish

1. Preheat the oven to 500°F.

2. Fill a large pot three-quarters full with water, place over high heat, and bring to a boil. Add the broccoli rabe and blanch for 1 minute. Drain well.

3. In a large skillet over high heat, warm the oil. Add the garlic and cook for 1 minute. Add the broccoli rabe, raisins, and red pepper flakes and sauté until the broccoli is tender, about 5 minutes. Season with salt.

4. While the broccoli is cooking, toast the bread slices in the oven until golden, about 5 minutes. Pile ⅓ cup of ricotta on top of each slice and top with the broccoli rabe mixture. Serve, garnished with the grated cheese.

CARROT LEEK SOUP

FRESHLY DUG SPRING CARROTS HAVE BRIGHT, THIN SKINS, WHICH ARE NOT BITTER LIKE THE SKINS OF OLDER STORAGE CARROTS. YOU CAN SKIP PEELING THESE TENDER ROOTS IF YOU'VE GOT THEM.

YIELD: 4 TO 6 SERVINGS

2 tablespoons unsalted butter

1 tablespoon extra-virgin olive oil

2 medium leeks, white and tender greens parts only, cleaned (see below) and sliced

2 pounds baby carrots, scrubbed and sliced

1 large sprig of tarragon

1 teaspoon coarse sea salt or kosher salt, plus additional to taste

Juice of 1 orange

1 tablespoon maple syrup or honey

Freshly milled black pepper

1. In a pressure cooker over medium heat, melt 1 tablespoon of the butter with the oil. Add the leeks and sauté until translucent, about 2 minutes.

2. Add 1 quart of water, the carrots, sprig of tarragon, and 1 teaspoon of salt. Secure the lid, and bring to full pressure over high heat. Cook the carrots for 7 minutes. Transfer the pot to the sink and run cold water over it to release the pressure.

3. Discard the sprig of tarragon. Add the orange juice, maple syrup, and remaining tablespoon of butter. Using an immersion blender puree the soup (or transfer in batches to a standard blender or watertight food processor). Season with salt and pepper.

TO CLEAN LEEKS

First cut off the roots end and the tough greens. Make a few vertical slices through the pale green upper part of the trimmed leek, but do not cut through the base. Swish the cut end in a bowl of water. The grit will settle on the bottom of the bowl. Then drain, pat dry, and slice.

MENU 11

•

ORZO WITH
MUSTARD GREENS

•

WARM CHICKPEA SALAD
WITH SHALLOTS AND
RED WINE VINAIGRETTE

MARKET LIST

FRESH PRODUCE

1 pound red mustard
greens, or another quick-
cooking green, such as
green mustard, baby
spinach, or a mild arugula

1 large carrot

1 large or 2 medium
shallots

Garlic

Flat-leaf parsley

1 lemon

DAIRY

Unsalted butter

4 to 6 ounces Asiago
cheese

PANTRY

Extra-virgin olive oil

Red wine vinegar

12 ounces orzo pasta

2 (15-ounce) cans
chickpeas

Coarse sea salt or
kosher salt

Black peppercorns

EQUIPMENT

Large pot

Medium saucepan

Box grater

Colander

Citrus zester

MENU 11 GAME PLAN

1. Bring a large pot of water
   to a boil.
2. Bring a medium saucepan
   of water to a boil.
3. Make chickpea salad.
4. Prepare the orzo with
   mustard greens.
5. Serve the orzo with
   chickpea salad on
   the side.

ORZO WITH MUSTARD GREENS

IN THE SPRING, CRUCIFEROUS LEAFY GREENS SUCH AS
MUSTARD GREENS, TURNIP TOPS, AND EVEN BROCCOLI AND
CAULIFLOWER LEAVES, ARE SO TENDER THAT THEY REQUIRE
ONLY A BRIEF SAUTÉ TO BRING OUT THEIR MUSKY CHARM.
TENDER RED MUSTARD GREENS ARE EASY TO COME BY AT
FARMER'S MARKETS. IF YOU CAN'T GET THEM, YOU CAN
SUBSTITUTE ANOTHER QUICK-COOKING GREEN, SUCH AS GREEN
MUSTARD, BABY SPINACH, OR A MILD VARIETY OF ARUGULA.

YIELD: 4 SERVINGS

2 tablespoons coarse sea salt or
    kosher salt, plus additional to taste
1½ cups orzo
2 tablespoons unsalted butter
1 pound red mustard greens,
    chopped
Grated zest of 1 lemon
Freshly milled black pepper
1 cup freshly grated Asiago cheese
    for garnish

1. Fill a large pot three-quarters full with water, place over high heat, and bring to a boil. Add 2 tablespoons of salt. When the water returns to a boil, stir in the orzo and cook until al dente. Drain well.

2. Return the cooked orzo to the pot, stir in the butter, and place over high heat. Add the mustard greens and lemon zest and cook, stirring until the greens wilt, 3 to 5 minutes. Season with salt and pepper. Serve the pasta with freshly grated cheese on top.

WARM CHICKPEA SALAD WITH SHALLOTS AND RED WINE VINAIGRETTE

SIMMERING CANNED BEANS IN LIGHTLY SALTED WATER FOR SEVERAL MINUTES FRESHENS THEM UP. THE WARMED BEANS ALSO ABSORB BETTER THE FLAVORS OF THE VINAIGRETTE.

YIELD: 4 SERVINGS

1 large or 2 medium shallots, thinly sliced
3 tablespoons red wine vinegar
1 garlic clove, minced
¼ teaspoon coarse sea salt or kosher
    salt, plus additional to taste
2 (15-ounce) cans chickpeas, drained
1 large carrot, peeled and coarsely
    grated
½ cup flat-leaf parsley leaves,
    chopped
⅓ cup extra-virgin olive oil
Freshly milled black pepper

1. In a large bowl, combine the shallots, vinegar, garlic, and salt. Set aside for 10 minutes to allow the shallots and garlic to mellow.

2. In a medium saucepan over high heat, bring 2 quarts of water to a boil. Add the chickpeas and blanch for 1 to 2 minutes. Drain.

3. Add the carrot, parsley, and oil to the shallot mixture. Toss in the chickpeas and season with salt and pepper. Serve immediately.

MENU 12

•

SESAME NOODLES WITH TOFU STEAKS AND BABY ASIAN GREENS

•

PEA SHOOT AND SPROUT SALAD

MARKET LIST

FRESH PRODUCE
3 to 4 ounces pea shoots
1 cup sunflower sprouts
1 pound baby bok choy
Scallions
1 lemon

PERISHABLES
1 ½ pounds firm or
    extra-firm tofu
8 ounces kimchee

PANTRY
Extra-virgin olive oil
Neutral oil, such as
    canola, grapeseed, or
    sunflower
Toasted sesame oil
Soy sauce
Mirin
Sesame seeds
12 ounces udon or soba
    noodles or Chinese
    style wheat noodles
Crushed red pepper flakes
Honey
Coarse sea salt or
    kosher salt

EQUIPMENT
Large pot with lid
Large nonstick skillet
Colander
Wire whisk
Citrus juicer

MENU 12 GAME PLAN

1. Bring a large pot of water to a boil.
2. Prepare the sesame noodles with tofu steaks through step 4.
3. Rinse and drain the bok choy and set aside.
4. Trim and slice the scallion.
5. Prepare the salad.
6. Steam the bok choy.
7. Finish the sesame noodles.
8. Divide the noodles among 4 bowls, topping each with a slab of tofu and a portion of greens. Sprinkle with scallions.
9. Serve with the salad and kimchee.

SESAME NOODLES WITH TOFU STEAKS AND BABY ASIAN GREENS

YIELD: **4** SERVINGS

1½ pounds firm or extra-firm
   tofu, cut into 12 equal slices
7 tablespoons soy sauce
3 tablespoons mirin (see page 135)
3 tablespoons honey
1 teaspoon crushed red pepper flakes
2 tablespoons neutral oil, such as
   grapeseed, canola, or sunflower
¾ pound udon or soba noodles
2 tablespoons sesame seeds,
   toasted (see page 7)
2 tablespoons toasted sesame oil
1 pound baby bok choy, rinsed well but not trimmed
1 cup kimchee
1 scallion, thinly sliced

1. Fill a large pot three-quarters full with water and place over high heat. Bring to a boil, and keep the water at a boil while you prepare the tofu.

2. Lay the tofu slices on one half of a clean cloth towel. Fold the other half over the tofu and gently press down to extract any excess moisture.

3. Place 6 tablespoons of the soy sauce, the mirin, honey, and red pepper flakes in a small bowl and whisk to combine.

4. Warm a large nonstick skillet over high heat and add the neutral oil. Let it heat for 30 seconds. Add the tofu and fry until golden brown on the bottom, about 3 minutes. Flip the pieces over, pour on the soy mixture, and cook until the sauce has reduced and thickened, another 5 minutes.

5. Meanwhile, add the noodles to the boiling water and cook according to the package instructions until done. Drain the noodles, and transfer them to a large bowl. Add the sesame seeds, sesame oil, and remaining soy sauce, tossing the pasta to blend well.

6. Return the pot to high heat and add the bok choy and 1 cup of water. Cover the pot and steam until the bok choy is crisp-tender and bright green, about 2 minutes. Serve the noodles topped with greens and tofu, sprinkled with scallions. Accompany with kimchee and the pea shoot salad.

PEA SHOOT AND SPROUT SALAD

PEA SHOOTS, THOSE DELICATE, CRUNCHY, SWEET MICROGREENS, ARE THE TENDRILS AND UPPERMOST LEAVES OF THE PEA PLANT. HERE I COMBINE THEM WITH SUNFLOWER SPROUTS, WHICH ARE VERY SUCCULENT AND CRISP. IT'S A GREAT COMBINATION.

YIELD: 4 SERVINGS

2 tablespoons extra-virgin olive oil
1 tablespoon freshly squeezed lemon juice
Coarse sea salt or kosher salt
4 cups pea shoots
1 cup sunflower sprouts, roots trimmed

1. In a salad bowl, whisk together the oil and lemon juice. Season with salt.

2. Add the pea shoots and sunflower sprouts and toss to combine.

SPRING

Warm Honey Lemon Curd
over Strawberries

Mango Lime Fool with Dates

Almond Shortbread Cookies

Maple Rhubarb Compote with
Crystallized Ginger

Strawberry Buttermilk Soup

Roasted Cherries in Red Wine

Rhubarb Crisp

DESSERTS

WARM HONEY LEMON CURD OVER STRAWBERRIES

LEFTOVER LEMON CURD IS TERRIFIC ON TOAST. IT
WILL KEEP IN THE FRIDGE FOR UP TO A WEEK.

YIELD: **4** SERVINGS

4 large eggs
½ cup sugar, preferably organic
  washed cane sugar (see page 8)
5 tablespoons freshly squeezed lemon juice
¼ cup honey
1½ teaspoons grated lemon zest
Pinch of fine sea salt
6 tablespoons unsalted butter, cut into pieces
1 pint strawberries, hulled and quartered

1. In a heavy, medium-sized saucepan over low heat, whisk together the eggs, sugar, lemon juice, honey, lemon zest, and salt and bring to a simmer, stirring constantly.

2. Add the butter and continue to cook, stirring, until the lemon curd is thick enough to coat the back of a wooden spoon, about 5 minutes.

3. Strain the lemon curd through a sieve and serve warm over the strawberries.

MANGO LIME FOOL
WITH DATES

MAKE SURE TO USE VERY RIPE, SOFT MANGOES FOR THIS
RECIPE. IF MANGOES ARE UNAVAILABLE,
SUBSTITUTE RIPE BANANAS OR PAPAYAS.

YIELD: **4** SERVINGS

1 cup labneh yogurt (see page 139)
   or sour cream
½ cup heavy cream
3 tablespoons sugar, preferably
   organic washed cane sugar
   (see page 8), or to taste
2 ripe mangoes, peeled and
   coarsely chopped
2 teaspoons freshly squeezed lime juice
4 pitted dates, thinly sliced
2 tablespoons chopped toasted
   pistachios (optional, see page 7)

1. In a medium bowl, whisk the labneh to loosen it. In another medium bowl, beat the cream with 1 ½ tablespoons of the sugar just until it thickens (it should not be thick enough to hold peaks). Fold the whipped cream into the labneh.

2. In a blender or food processor, combine the mangoes, lime juice, and the remaining 1 ½ tablespoons of sugar, and puree. Add more sugar to taste, if desired. Add the mango mixture to the labneh cream and fold until they are partially combined.

3. Spoon the fool into 4 glasses and chill until ready to serve. Garnish with the dates and pistachios if desired.

ALMOND SHORTBREAD COOKIES

HERE IS A FLAT-OUT YUMMY COOKIE THAT SATISFIES
THE UNIVERSAL DESIRE FOR CRUNCH.

YIELD: **6** SERVINGS

¼ cup whole almonds, unpeeled
1 cup all-purpose flour
⅓ cup sugar, preferably organic washed
    cane sugar (see page 8)
Pinch of salt
½ cup (1 stick) unsalted butter, cut into pieces
1 teaspoon vanilla extract

1. Preheat the oven to 350°F.

2. In the bowl of a food processor, pulse the almonds until finely chopped. Add the flour, sugar, and salt, and process until the nuts are finely ground. Add the butter and vanilla and pulse until the mixture comes together in a ball.

3. Place the dough on a baking sheet and pat it into a 9-inch round, about ⅛ inch thick. Use a fork to prick the dough all over. With a knife, score the dough (cut it part way through) into 6 wedges.

4. Bake until the shortbread is golden brown around the edges, about 12 to 15 minutes. Let cool, then break into wedges. Serve with Strawberry Buttermilk Soup (see page 76) or Roasted Cherries in Red Wine (see page 77).

MAPLE RHUBARB COMPOTE
WITH CRYSTALLIZED GINGER

YIELD: **4** SERVINGS

1 pound rhubarb, trimmed and cut
　　crosswise into ¾-inch pieces (about 3 cups)
⅓ cup chopped crystallized ginger
½ cup pure maple syrup
¾ crème fraîche or sour cream for
　　serving

1. In a large skillet over high heat, combine the rhubarb, ginger, and maple syrup and bring to a boil. Reduce the heat and simmer until the rhubarb is tender, but not falling apart, about 5 to 7 minutes.

2. Cool slightly, and serve in bowls with crème fraîche or sour cream.

STRAWBERRY
BUTTERMILK SOUP

THIS SUPERLIGHT DESSERT IS IRRESISTIBLE ON A HOT
SUMMER EVENING. BUTTERMILK SMOOTHS OUT THE BRIGHT
BERRY FLAVOR WHILE BRINGING OUT ITS SWEETNESS.

YIELD: **4** SERVINGS

2 pints strawberries, hulled
⅔ cup buttermilk
⅓ cup sugar, preferably organic washed
　　cane sugar (see page 8)
3 to 4 ice cubes
Shortbread cookies for serving (optional)

1. Slice 4 strawberries and set them aside for garnish. In a blender or food processor, combine the remaining strawberries, the buttermilk, sugar, and ice. Puree until smooth.

2. Spoon the soup into 4 small serving bowls and garnish with the reserved strawberry slices. Serve with shortbread cookies if desired.

ROASTED CHERRIES IN RED WINE

THIS IS ESPECIALLY GOOD WITH VANILLA ICE CREAM OR FROZEN YOGURT

YIELD: **4** TO **6** SERVINGS

¾ cup dry red wine, such as Côtes
    du Rhône, Zinfandel, or Pinot Noir
¼ cup sugar, preferably organic
    washed cane sugar (see page 8)
1 bay leaf
1 ½ pounds cherries, stemmed
1 tablespoon unsalted butter, cut into pieces

1. Preheat the oven to 450°F.

2. In a small saucepan over high heat, bring the red wine, sugar, and bay leaf to a boil. Reduce the heat to low and simmer for 5 minutes.

3. Arrange the cherries in a 10-inch gratin dish or cake pan (or another pan that will hold them snugly in one layer). Pour the wine syrup over the cherries and dot them with the butter.

4. Roast the cherries, stirring occasionally, for 15 minutes. Serve warm or at room temperature.

SPEED TIP

Don't bother stemming the cherries if you're in a hurry. They give the finished dish attitude and make it fun to eat.

RHUBARB CRISP

LEFTOVERS ARE GREAT FOR BREAKFAST; JUST
SUBSTITUTE YOGURT FOR THE WHIPPED CREAM.

YIELD: 4 TO 6 SERVINGS

1½ pounds rhubarb, trimmed and
    sliced (about 4½ cups)
¾ cup sugar, preferably organic
    washed cane sugar (see page 8)
1 teaspoon grated orange zest
¾ cup all-purpose flour
¼ cup brown sugar, preferably Demerara (see page 8)
½ teaspoon ground cinnamon
Pinch of kosher or fine sea salt
7 tablespoons cold unsalted butter, cut into pieces
Whipped cream for serving

1. Position a rack in the center of the over and preheat to 425°F.

2. In a large saucepan over medium-high heat, combine the rhubarb, sugar, and orange zest and simmer for 5 minutes, until the rhubarb is tender.

3. Meanwhile, in a food processor or medium bowl, combine the flour, brown sugar, cinnamon, and salt. Pulse or mix to combine. Add the butter and pulse or use two knives to cut the butter into the flour mixture. The mixture should resemble very coarse crumbs with pea-sized bits of butter.

4. Transfer the rhubarb mixture to a 9-inch pie plate or 10-inch gratin dish and sprinkle the brown sugar topping over it. Bake until the topping is golden brown, about 25 minutes. Serve warm with whipped cream.

SUMMER

Ascension. . . . A time for fruiting. A riot of cucumbers, squash, melons, tomatoes, peppers, and eggplants. Farm stands groaning under the weight of fresh-picked corn, tender summer broccoli, and lush blackberries. The porous, ruby fruit of watermelons. Squash vines spreading outward, threatening to take over the garden. Butter melting on sweet, milky ears of corn. Plants rush toward you, shouting pick me, cook me, share me. Peaches are heavy as the moon at high tide—bite into them and juice flows down your chin. Life is full and beautiful. Who can be patient at this time of year? Tomatoes ripen urgently, berries distill sweetness, pleasure comes easily.

SUMMER MENUS

1. Black Bean and Zucchini Quesadillas
   Chilled Cucumber Soup with Mint

2. Cucumber Salad
   Spicy Corn Frittata with Tomatoes and Scallions

3. Seared Tofu with Spicy Black Beans and Mango Salsa
   Chilled Avocado Soup with Lime and Jalapeño

4. Chilled Tomato Soup with Shallots, Cucumbers, and Corn
   Warm Green Beans and New Potatoes with Sliced Eggs and Grilled Onions

5. Three Sisters Stew with Okra and Leeks
   Arepas: Pan-Grilled Colombian Corn Cakes

6. Bruschetta with Goat Cheese, Olives, Tomatoes and Thyme
   Lentil and Corn Salad with Sweet Peppers and Basil

7. Cracked Wheat
   Tempeh Ratatouille

8. Whole Grain Pasta with Salsa Cruda
   **White Bean and Arugula Salad with
   Lemon Dill Vinaigrette**

9. Asian Cucumber Salad
   **Thai-Style Tofu and Vegetables
   in Spicy Coconut Broth with
   Jasmine Rice**

10. Spicy Summer Bean and Chickpea
    Salad with Harissa Vinaigrette
    **Fresh Corn Polenta with Sautéed
    Cherry Tomatoes**

11. Pita Pizza with Green Olives,
    Monterey Jack, and Chopped Salad
    **Pan-Seared Summer Squash with
    Garlic and Mint**

12. Edamame
    **Chilled Soba Noodles in Dashi with
    Tofu and Shredded Romaine**

MENU 1

•

BLACK BEAN AND ZUCCHINI QUESADILLAS

•

CHILLED CUCUMBER SOUP WITH MINT

MARKET LIST

FRESH PRODUCE
2 pounds zucchini
3 large cucumbers
  (1 ½ pounds)
1 jalapeño pepper
Scallions
Garlic
Mint

DAIRY
8 ounces plain whole-milk
  yogurt
12 ounces Monterey Jack
  cheese

PANTRY
Extra-virgin olive oil
Red wine vinegar
Tomato salsa, purchased
  or the ingredients for
  homemade
  (see page 87)
8 flour tortillas (8 inches
  in diameter)
2 (15-ounce) cans black
  beans
Coarse sea salt or
  kosher salt
Black peppercorns

EQUIPMENT
1 large or 2 6-inch skillets
Blender
Box grater
Colander

MENU 1 GAME PLAN
1. Prepare the soup and
   chill it.
2. If you are making your
   own salsa, now is a good
   time to do so.
3. Prepare the quesadillas.
4. Serve the soup with
   quesadillas and salsa on
   the side.

SPEED TIP
Use 2 small skillets at the
same time when you fry
or toast quesadillas,
pancakes, or arepas.

BLACK BEAN AND ZUCCHINI QUESADILLAS

A GOOD QUESADILLA FRESH OFF THE SKILLET OFFERS SOME OF THE FINER PLEASURES IN LIFE: CRUNCH, OOZE, SALT, AND SPICE. . . . ANYBODY HUNGRY?

YIELD: 4 SERVINGS

2 pounds zucchini, coarsely grated
1½ teaspoons coarse sea salt or
    kosher salt, plus additional to taste
2 (15-ounce) cans black beans,
    drained
12 ounces grated Monterey Jack
    cheese, coarsely grated
2 scallions, chopped
1 jalapeño pepper, with seeds, finely chopped
8 flour tortillas (8 inches in diameter)
Extra-virgin olive oil for brushing the tortillas
Chipotle Salsa, (recipe follows) or
    store-bought tomato salsa

1. In a colander, toss together the grated zucchini and salt with your hands. Squeeze the zucchini to remove a lot of its liquid.

2. In a large bowl, combine the zucchini, beans, cheese, scallions, and jalapeño.

3. Brush 4 of the tortillas with oil on one side. Turn over the tortillas so the oiled side is on the bottom. Divide the bean mixture between the tortillas, spreading it to the edges. Top each with a plain tortilla and brush the top with oil.

4. Warm a large skillet over medium heat. Place a quesadilla in the pan and cook until the cheese melts and the tortillas are golden brown, about 3 minutes per side. Repeat with the remaining quesadillas. If you have two skillets, use them both to cook the quesadillas more quickly. (Alternately, arrange the quesadillas on a rimmed baking sheet and broil, about 6 inches from the heat source, until the cheese melts and the quesadillas are golden brown, about 1 to 2 minutes per side.) Serve with salsa.

CHILLED CUCUMBER SOUP WITH MINT

IF YOU WANT TO SERVE THIS IMMEDIATELY AFTER BLENDING, ADD AN ICE CUBE OR TWO TO THE BLENDER TO CHILL IT DOWN. USING CUCUMBERS AND YOGURT STRAIGHT FROM THE FRIDGE ALSO KEEPS THINGS COOL.

YIELD: **4** SERVINGS

3 large cucumbers (1½ pounds), peeled

1 cup plain whole-milk yogurt

1½ tablespoons extra-virgin olive oil

2 teaspoons red wine vinegar

1 tablespoon chopped fresh mint

1 garlic clove, peeled

1½ teaspoons coarse sea salt or kosher salt

Freshly milled black pepper

1. Halve the cucumbers lengthwise. Scoop out their seeds with a spoon and discard. Coarsely chop the cucumber and transfer to a blender.

2. Add the yogurt, olive oil, vinegar, mint, garlic, and salt and blend until smooth. Season with a little black pepper. Chill until ready to serve.

SOMETHING EXTRA: CHIPOTLE SALSA

THERE ARE PLENTY OF GOOD COMMERCIAL SALSAS AVAILABLE THAT YOU CAN USE IN A PINCH, BUT IF YOU HAVE THE TIME, MAKING YOUR OWN IS WELL WORTH IT.

YIELD: **4** SERVINGS

5 to 6 ripe plum tomatoes, cored, seeded and diced

½ cup chopped fresh cilantro

⅓ cup chopped red onion

1 chipotle chile in adobo sauce, drained if desired, and finely chopped

Juice of 1 lime

Coarse sea salt or kosher salt

In a small bowl, toss together all the ingredients. Add some of the adobo sauce if you desire a hotter salsa.

MENU 2

•

CUCUMBER SALAD

•

SPICY CORN FRITTATA WITH
TOMATOES
AND SCALLIONS

MARKET LIST

FRESH PRODUCE

2 large or 3 medium ears
  sweet corn
2 large ripe tomatoes
1 ½ pounds Kirby
  cucumbers
1 jalapeño pepper
1 bunch scallions
1 head garlic
1 medium or 2 small red
  onions
1 large bunch cilantro
Dill
Rosemary

DAIRY

Unsalted butter
8 large eggs

PANTRY

Extra-virgin olive oil
Cider vinegar
Crushed red pepper
  flakes
Sugar
Coarse sea salt or
  kosher salt
Black peppercorns
1 loaf crusty country
  bread

EQUIPMENT

Large ovenproof skillet
  (preferably nonstick)
  with lid
Rimmed baking sheet

MENU 2 GAME PLAN

1. Set a rack on the top
   shelf of the oven and
   preheat to 450°F.
2. Prepare the cucumber
   salad through step 2.
3. Make the frittata.
4. Make the garlic toasts.
5. Finish the cucumber
   salad.
6. Serve wedges of
   frittata accompanied
   by cucumber salad and
   garlic toasts.

CUCUMBER SALAD

PERSONALLY, I CAN'T STAND RAW ONIONS IN SALADS. THEY
TEND TO COMPLETELY OVERWHELM WHATEVER THEY COME
IN CONTACT WITH. HERE I USE A METHOD THAT TAMES THEIR
FIRE AND TRANSFORMS THEM INTO CHARMING, LIGHTLY
PICKLED, SWEET-AND-SOUR CRUNCHY RINGS WITH A
SPARKLING IRIDESCENCE THAT REALLY DRESSES UP THE
RATHER BLAND PERSONALITY OF CUCUMBERS.

YIELD: 4 SERVINGS

1½ pounds Kirby cucumbers, thinly
    sliced (about 8 cucumbers)
1 teaspoon plus 1 tablespoon coarse sea
    salt or kosher salt
2 tablespoons cider vinegar
1 tablespoon sugar, preferably organic
    washed cane sugar (see page 8)
1 medium or 2 small red onions, sliced
    into thin rings
2 tablespoons minced fresh dill
1 tablespoon extra-virgin olive oil
Freshly milled black pepper

1. In a medium bowl, toss the cucumbers with 1 teaspoon of
the salt. Refrigerate for 30 minutes.

2. In another medium bowl, whisk 1 cup of water with the
vinegar, sugar, and remaining tablespoon of salt. Stir in the
onions and refrigerate for 30 minutes.

3. Drain the cucumbers and transfer them to a salad bowl.
Lift the onions from their marinade and combine them with
the cucumbers. Reserve the marinade.

4. Season the salad with some of the onion marinade and
toss with the dill, oil, and pepper.

SMALL KIRBY

or pickling cucumbers
are my choice for this
salad. They have a
thinner skin and smaller
seeds than the common
larger English variety. If
Kirby cucumbers are
unavailable, English
ones will work well if
they are peeled and
seeded. Peel a few
strips of skin from the
cucumbers, leaving on
dark green stripes
of skin for decoration.
Trim the ends and slice
lengthwise in half. Use
a teaspoon to scoop
out the seeds and
discard them. Slice the
cucumber crosswise
into ¼-inch-thick slices.

SPICY CORN FRITTATA WITH TOMATOES AND SCALLIONS

FRITTATAS ARE TRADITIONALLY SERVED AT ROOM
TEMPERATURE, BUT THIS ONE IS ALSO GOOD HOT,
STRAIGHT FROM THE PAN.

YIELD: 4 SERVINGS

¼ cup extra-virgin olive oil

2 large ripe tomatoes, cored,
   seeded, and chopped (about 2 cups)

2 large or 3 medium ears sweet
   corn, kernels scraped off the cob
   (about 2 cups)

1 cup chopped fresh cilantro

1 bunch scallions, trimmed and sliced

2 garlic cloves, finely chopped

1 jalapeño pepper, seeded and finely chopped

Coarse sea salt or kosher salt and freshly
   milled black pepper

8 large eggs

1 tablespoon cold unsalted butter,
   cut into small pieces

1. Set a rack on the top shelf of the oven and preheat to 450°F.

2. In a large ovenproof skillet over high heat, warm 2 tablespoons of the oil. Add the tomatoes and sauté for 2 minutes. Add the corn, cilantro, scallions, garlic, and jalapeño and sauté for 2 more minutes, or until the garlic is fragrant and the mixture thickens. Transfer the vegetables to a plate and let cool for several minutes. Season with salt and pepper.

3. In a large bowl, season the eggs with salt and pepper. Whisk lightly with a fork—only enough to mix the whites and yolks. Add the sautéed vegetables and butter and stir to combine.

4. Wipe out the skillet with a paper towel and place over medium heat. Add the remaining 2 tablespoons of oil and swirl all around and up the sides of the pan.

5. Add the egg and vegetable mixture and stir gently with the back of a fork without touching the bottom or sides of the pan. Cover the pan, lower the heat, and cook for 1 to 2 minutes, until the bottom of the frittata begins to set. Transfer the pan (uncovered) to the top shelf of the oven and bake until golden brown and puffed, about 10 minutes.

6. Slide the frittata onto a serving platter, cut into wedges, and serve immediately or cool to room temperature.

SOMETHING EXTRA: GARLIC TOASTS

WHY HAVE PLAIN BREAD (EVEN IF IT IS A GREAT ARTISANAL SOURDOUGH LOAF) WHEN YOU CAN HAVE SOMETHING TRULY SPECIAL? HERE, A SIMPLE GARLIC AND HERB OIL TURNS THE ORDINARY INTO THE MEMORABLE. IF YOU DON'T HAVE ROSEMARY, TRY SAGE, THYME, BASIL, OR PARSLEY INSTEAD.

½ cup extra-virgin olive oil
4 garlic cloves, peeled and crushed with the side of a knife
1 tablespoon chopped fresh rosemary
1 teaspoon crushed red pepper flakes
1 loaf crusty country bread, cut into ½-inch-thick slices
Coarse sea salt or kosher salt

1. Preheat the oven to 450°F.

2. In a small bowl, combine the oil, garlic, rosemary, and red pepper flakes and set aside.

3. Arrange the bread slices on a rimmed baking sheet and toast them in the oven for 5 minutes.

4. Spread the toasted slices liberally with the garlic oil and sprinkle with salt.

5. Return to the oven and bake until golden brown and fragrant, about 10 minutes. Serve immediately.

MENU 3

•

SEARED TOFU WITH
SPICY BLACK BEANS
AND MANGO SALSA

•

CHILLED AVOCADO
SOUP WITH LIME
AND JALAPEÑO

MARKET LIST

FRESH PRODUCE
3 ripe avocados
1 medium tomato
2 jalapeño peppers
1 large red onion
Garlic
Cilantro
3 limes
2 lemons
2 ripe mangoes
Ginger

DAIRY AND SOY
16 ounces sour cream
1 pound extra-firm tofu

PANTRY
Extra-virgin olive oil
Cumin seeds
12 ounces white rice
    (basmati, jasmine, or
    sushi)
1 (15-ounce) can black
    beans
1 flour tortilla (8 inches)
Coarse sea salt or
    kosher salt
Black peppercorns

EQUIPMENT
Large skillet or sauté pan
Large nonstick skillet
Small saucepan with lid
Blender
Spice mill
Citrus juicer

MENU 3 GAME PLAN
1. Prepare the soup through
   step 2.
2. Make the salsa, reserving
   some extra chopped
   cilantro to garnish
   the soup.
3. Cook the rice.
4. Fry the tortilla strips for
   the soup garnish.
5. Saute the onions with
   seasonings for the black
   beans and simmer the
   black beans.
6. Sear the tofu.
7. Finish the soup.
8. Finish the tofu.
9. Serve the tofu and soup.

SEARED TOFU WITH SPICY BLACK BEANS AND MANGO SALSA

THE COMPONENTS OF THIS MENU ALL WORK WELL TOGETHER, BUT IF YOU JUST WANT TO MAKE THE BEANS AND SALSA AND HAVE THEM WITH CORN CHIPS, THAT'S FINE TOO.

YIELD: 4 SERVINGS

For the rice

1½ cups white rice (basmati, jasmine, or sushi), rinsed

¾ teaspoon coarse sea salt or kosher salt

For the black beans

¼ cup extra-virgin olive oil

1 cup diced red onion

2 teaspoons cumin seeds, toasted and ground (see page 8), or 2 teaspoons ground cumin

2 tablespoons grated fresh ginger

2 garlic cloves, minced

1 (15-ounce) can black beans

For the tofu

1 pound extra-firm tofu, cut into 4 thick slices

Coarse sea salt or kosher salt

For the salsa

2 ripe mangoes, peeled and diced

1 medium tomato, cored, seeded, and diced

¼ cup chopped fresh cilantro, plus additional for garnish

3 tablespoons freshly squeezed lemon juice

2 tablespoons minced red onion

1 jalapeño pepper, with seeds, minced

1¼ teaspoons extra-virgin olive oil

Pinch of coarse sea salt or kosher salt

1. To make the rice, in a small saucepan, bring 2 ¼ cups of water to a boil. Add the rice and salt, cover, and simmer over low heat for 20 minutes. Fluff with a fork before serving.

2. To prepare the beans, in a large skillet, warm the oil over medium heat. Add the onion and cumin and sauté for 5 minutes. Add the ginger and garlic and sauté for 2 more minutes. Add the beans with their liquid and simmer until thickened, about 5 minutes.

3. To prepare the tofu, warm a large nonstick skillet over high heat. Add the tofu to the pan and sprinkle it with salt. Cook until browned on each side, about 3 minutes per side.

4. Meanwhile, make the salsa: In a medium bowl, combine the mangoes, tomato, cilantro, lemon juice, onion, jalapeño, oil, and salt; mix to combine.

5. To serve, spoon some of the beans and rice onto each of 4 plates, and top with the tofu and salsa. Garnish with cilantro.

CHILLED AVOCADO SOUP WITH LIME AND JALAPEÑO

THIS CREAMY, MOUSSELIKE AVOCADO SOUP CAN BE SERVED WITH TOMATO TORTILLAS FOR AN EXCELLENT COLOR CONTRAST. YOU CAN MAKE IT A DAY AHEAD OF TIME; THE LIME JUICE WILL PRESERVE THE SOUP'S BRIGHT COLOR.

YIELD: 4 SERVINGS

3 limes
3 ripe avocados, peeled and pitted
1 garlic clove, chopped
½ small jalapeño pepper, with
    seeds, chopped
1 teaspoon coarse sea salt or
    kosher salt, plus additional to taste
2½ tablespoons extra-virgin
    olive oil
1 large flour tortilla (8 inches), cut into
    2-inch x ¼-inch strips
Sour cream for serving
Chopped fresh cilantro for garnish

1. Squeeze the juice from 2 ½ of the limes and cut the remaining half into 4 wedges for garnish.

2. In a blender, combine 3 cups of ice water (a mixture of water and ice) with the lime juice, avocados, garlic, jalapeño, and the salt and blend until smooth. Chill the soup until ready to serve.

3. Heat the oil in a large skillet or sauté pan over medium heat. Add the tortilla strips and fry until they are crunchy and golden-brown, about 2 minutes. Drain the strips on paper towels and sprinkle them with salt.

4. Spoon the soup into bowls, and place a dollop of sour cream in the center of each bowl, top with tortilla strips, and garnish with cilantro. Serve with lime wedges on the side.

MENU 4

•

CHILLED TOMATO SOUP
WITH SHALLOTS,
CUCUMBERS, AND CORN

•

WARM GREEN BEANS
AND NEW POTATOES
WITH SLICED EGGS
AND GRILLED ONIONS

MARKET LIST

FRESH PRODUCE
3 pounds tomatoes
1 ear of corn
1 cucumber
1 pound green beans
2 pounds small new
    potatoes (red, yellow,
    or white, or any
    combination)
1 large shallot
1 large red onion
Fresh herbs: basil,
    tarragon, chives, or
    parsley (one or any
    combination)
Thyme
1 lemon

DAIRY
4 large eggs

PANTRY
Extra-virgin olive oil
Red wine vinegar
Balsamic vinegar
Whole grain mustard
Coarse sea salt or
    kosher salt
Black peppercorns
1 loaf country bread

EQUIPMENT
Large saucepan
Medium stockpot with lid
Large cast-iron skillet,
    heavy sauté pan,
    griddle, or grill pan
Steamer basket to fit in
    the stockpot
Sieve
Food processor or
    blender
Wire whisk

MENU 4 GAME PLAN
1. Preheat the oven to
   325°F.
2. Boil a large pot of water
   for the two dishes.
3. Prepare the soup through
   step 2.
4. Sauté the onions for the
   salad.
5. Marinate the onions in the
   vinaigrette.
6. Finish soup and chill it.
7. Warm a loaf of bread in
   the oven.
8. Finish the salad.
9. Serve the soup and salad
   with warm bread.

CHILLED TOMATO SOUP WITH SHALLOTS, CUCUMBERS, AND CORN

YOU MAY HAVE NOTICED THAT THERE ARE A LOT OF CHILLED SOUPS IN THIS CHAPTER. OF COURSE CHILLED SOUPS ARE A GREAT WAY TO EAT VEGETABLES IN THE SUMMER; THEY'RE SO REFRESHING AND REVIVING ON A HOT DAY. BUT THE KICKER IS THAT THEY'RE EVEN QUICKER TO PREPARE THAN SALADS— EVERYTHING GOES IN THE BLENDER AND IT'S DONE. THIS PARTICULAR SOUP, INSPIRED BY ALICE WATERS'S GAZPACHO, CAN ALSO BE SERVED AT ROOM TEMPERATURE OR EVEN WARM, AND IT IS ESPECIALLY GOOD WITH THICK SLICES OF BREAD.

YIELD: 4 SERVINGS

3 pounds tomatoes, roughly
    chopped
1 tablespoon coarse sea salt or
    kosher salt
1 large shallot, finely chopped
2 tablespoons red wine vinegar,
    plus additional to taste
1 ear of corn, shucked
1 cucumber
3 tablespoons chopped fresh basil,
    tarragon, parsley, or cilantro
    (one or any combination)

1. In a large bowl, toss the tomatoes with the salt and refrigerate for 20 minutes.

2. Meanwhile, in a small bowl, combine the shallot and 2 tablespoons of vinegar. Let sit for 15 minutes.

3. In a large saucepan, bring 3 quarts of lightly salted water to a boil. Add the corn and cook until tender, about 1 to 2 minutes. Transfer the corn to a plate and refrigerate until cool enough to handle. (Don't pour out the water, save it for the eggs and green beans in the next recipe.)

4. Peel the cucumber, halve it lengthwise, and use a teaspoon to scoop out the seeds. Cut the cucumber into ¼-inch cubes. Cut the kernels off the corncob.

5. In a food processor or blender, puree the tomatoes. Strain the liquid into a large bowl, discarding the solids. Use a slotted spoon or a fork to transfer the shallots to the tomato mixture. Stir in more of the vinegar to taste.

6. Stir the corn kernels, cucumber, and basil into the soup and serve cold or at room temperature.

WARM GREEN BEANS AND NEW POTATOES WITH SLICED EGGS AND GRILLED ONIONS

THE DRESSING FOR THIS WARM SALAD IS MADE WITH CARAMELIZED ONIONS, WHICH GIVES IT A UNIQUE SWEET-AND-TANGY FLAVOR.

YIELD: 4 SERVINGS

1 large red onion, peeled and cut into
    ½-inch crescents from root to stem
3 tablespoons balsamic vinegar
1 tablespoon whole grain mustard
1 teaspoon chopped fresh thyme leaves
3 tablespoons extra-virgin olive oil
Coarse sea salt or kosher salt and
    freshly milled black pepper
2 pounds small new potatoes, sliced ½-inch thick
4 large eggs
1 pound green beans, trimmed
Lemon wedges for serving

1. Warm a large, heavy skillet over medium heat for 3 minutes. Add the onion and cook, stirring occasionally, until deeply browned on all sides, about 8 to 10 minutes.

2. In a large salad bowl, whisk together the vinegar, mustard, and thyme. Whisk in the oil and season with salt and pepper. Add the cooked onions and toss to coat them with the vinaigrette.

3. In a stockpot fitted with a steamer insert, bring 1 inch of water to a boil. Add the potato slices and steam, covered, until tender, about 15 minutes. Transfer the potatoes to the bowl with the onions and toss gently to coat.

4. In a large saucepan, bring 3 quarts of water to a boil. Add the eggs, reduce the heat, and simmer for 10 minutes. Use a slotted spoon to transfer the cooked eggs to a bowl of cold water.

5. Add 1 tablespoon of salt to the water in the saucepan and return to a boil. Add the green beans and blanch until crisp-tender, about 2 to 3 minutes. Drain the beans, toss them with the onions and potatoes, and season with salt and pepper.

6. Peel and slice the cooled eggs and arrange them on top of the salad. Serve with lemon wedges on the side.

MENU 5

•

THREE SISTERS STEW
WITH OKRA AND LEEKS

•

AREPAS: PAN-GRILLED
COLOMBIAN CORN CAKES

MARKET LIST

FRESH PRODUCE
4 medium or 2 large leeks
1 beefsteak tomato or
   3 plum tomatoes
2 ears sweet corn
1 medium zucchini or
   summer squash
1 jalapeño pepper
8 to 10 okra pods
6 tomatillos
Cilantro

DAIRY
Unsalted butter
8 ounces sour cream
4 to 6 ounces queso
   fresco or mild French
   feta (see Note,
   page 107)

PANTRY
Extra-virgin olive oil
Cumin seeds
2 cups Mazteca (masa
   harina, see page 107)
1 (15-ounce) can pinto
   beans
Coarse sea salt or
   kosher salt
Black peppercorns

EQUIPMENT
Large nonstick skillet
   with lid
Dutch oven

MENU 5 GAME PLAN
1. Prepare the stew through
   step 1.
2. Prepare the corn cakes.
3. Season the stew and
   prepare the garnish.
4. Place a corn cake in each
   wide soup plate and ladle
   stew over it. Garnish with
   sour cream and chopped
   cilantro.

THREE SISTERS STEW WITH OKRA AND LEEKS

THE THREE SISTERS REPRESENT THE THREE DEITIES, OR
ENERGIES, MANIFESTED IN CORN, SQUASH, AND BEANS,
WHICH ARE THE FOUNDATION OF TRADITIONAL NATIVE
AMERICAN AGRICULTURE. IF OKRA IS UNAVAILABLE, MAKE
THIS STEW ANYWAY—IT'S TOO GOOD TO PASS UP.

YIELD: 4 TO 6 SERVINGS

4 medium or 2 large leeks, cleaned
   (see page 61) and white and tender
   green parts thinly sliced (about 2 cups)
2 tablespoons unsalted butter
2 tablespoons extra-virgin olive oil
1 jalapeño pepper, with seeds, thinly sliced
2 teaspoons coarse sea salt or
   kosher salt, plus additional to taste
1 teaspoon cumin seeds, toasted and ground
   (see page 8), or 1 teaspoon ground cumin
1 (15-ounce) can pinto beans
1 beefsteak tomato or 3 plum tomatoes,
   cored, seeded and roughly chopped
8 to 10 okra pods, cut crosswise into ¼-inch slices (about 1 cup)
2 ears sweet corn, kernels scraped off the cobs, and cobs reserved
1 medium zucchini or summer squash, sliced lengthwise
   and then cut crosswise into ½-inch pieces
6 tomatillos, husked and quartered
Freshly milled black pepper
Chopped cilantro for garnish
Sour cream for garnish

1. In a Dutch oven over high heat, combine the leeks, butter, oil, jalapeño, salt, and cumin. Sauté until the leeks soften, about 3 to 4 minutes. Add 6 cups of water, the beans and their liquid, tomato, okra, corn kernels, corncobs, squash, and tomatillos, and bring to a boil. Reduce the heat and simmer until the vegetables are tender, about 20 minutes.

2. Season with additional salt and fresh ground black pepper. Serve, garnished with cilantro and sour cream.

AREPAS: PAN-GRILLED COLOMBIAN CORN CAKES

MASA HARINA IS ONE OF THE OLDEST FAST FOODS. GROUND FROM PRECOOKED, CLEANED, DRY CORN THAT HAS BEEN COOKED IN LIME OR WOOD ASH, IT HAS FORMED THE STAPLE TORTILLA FOR CENTURIES. DUE TO ITS UNIQUE PROCESSING, THE CORN FLOUR, WHEN MOISTENED WITH WATER OR STOCK, IS EASILY MOLDED INTO ALL SORTS OF SHAPES, UNLIKE REGULAR GROUND CORNMEAL. MAZTECA IS THE BRAND I USE. THESE TRADITIONAL CORN CAKES WITH QUESO FRESCO ARE GREAT WITH ANY HEARTY SOUP OR STEW.

YIELD: 4 SERVINGS

2 cups masa harina
¼ cup (½ stick) unsalted butter, melted
½ cup queso fresco or mild French feta

1. In a medium bowl combine the masa harina, 1 ¾ cups cool water, and the melted butter and stir with a wooden spoon until the dough comes together in a mass. Kneed the dough in the bowl a few times with your hands until it is smooth. Cover the dough with a piece of plastic wrap or a damp towel and set aside for 5 minutes.

2. Warm a large, nonstick skillet over medium heat.

3. Uncover the dough and divide it in half. Divide each half into 4 equal pieces.

4. Form a piece of dough into a smooth patty. Put 2 tablespoons of cheese in the center and cover with a second piece of dough. Pat the dough together to form a smooth disk about 4 inches across. Repeat with the remaining dough to form 4 cakes.

5. Put the cakes in the skillet and cook, covered, for 5 minutes. Check after 3 minutes or so and lower the heat if necessary to prevent the cakes from burning. Flip the cakes and cook, uncovered, until both sides are speckled with brown spots, about 5 to 7 minutes.

QUESO FRESCO

is a truly vegetarian cheese, made simply from milk and lemon. Many cheeses are made with rennin (an enzyme derived from the stomach of a cow). You can substitute low-salt French or Bulgarian feta cheese. Or cover salty feta with milk and refrigerate overnight to leach out the salt. Drain and proceed with recipe.

MENU 6

●

BRUSCHETTA
WITH GOAT CHEESE,
OLIVES, TOMATOES,
AND THYME

●

LENTIL AND
CORN SALAD WITH
SWEET PEPPERS
AND BASIL

MARKET LIST

FRESH PRODUCE
1 bunch arugula
4 ears corn
1 red bell pepper
1 yellow bell pepper
½ pound green beans
4 medium ripe yet firm
   tomatoes
Scallions
Garlic
Basil
Thyme
1 lemon

DAIRY
8 ounces fresh goat
   cheese

PANTRY
Extra-virgin olive oil
Balsamic vinegar
Pearl barley
Lentils
Coarse sea salt or
   kosher salt
Black peppercorns
1 cup pitted oil-cured
   black olives
1 loaf country bread

EQUIPMENT
Large pot
Rimmed baking sheet
Wire whisk
Citrus juicer

MENU 6 GAME PLAN
1. Fill a large pot with
   3 quarts of water. Cover
   and place over high heat.
2. Set a rack on the middle
   shelf of the oven and
   preheat to 400°F.
3. Prepare the salad through
   step 2.
4. Prepare the bruschetta
   through step 2.
5. Finish the salad.
6. Finish the bruschetta.
7. Serve the bruschetta hot,
   accompanied by
   the salad.

BRUSCHETTA WITH GOAT CHEESE, OLIVES, TOMATOES, AND THYME

HERE'S ANOTHER MAIN COURSE BRUSCHETTA, THIS TIME MADE WITH GOAT CHEESE AND OLIVES.

YIELD: 4 SERVINGS

8 ounces fresh goat cheese
1 garlic clove, minced or crushed in a press
1 cup pitted kalamata or black oil-cured olives,
    rinsed and roughly chopped
¼ cup extra-virgin olive oil
Coarse sea salt or kosher salt and
    freshly milled black pepper
4 large, slices country bread,
    ¾ inch-thick
4 medium ripe yet firm tomatoes,
    sliced ¼-inch-thick
2 teaspoons minced fresh thyme
1 bunch arugula, washed and coarsely chopped
2 tablespoons balsamic vinegar

1. Preheat the oven to 400°F.

2. In a small bowl, combine the goat cheese, garlic, olives and 2 tablespoons of the olive oil and stir until smooth. Season with salt and pepper.

3. Arrange the bread on a rimmed baking sheet and toast until golden, about 5 minutes.

4. Arrange an oven rack 4 inches from the heat source and preheat the broiler.

5. Spread the toasts with the goat cheese mixture and top with the sliced tomatoes. Drizzle with the remaining olive oil and sprinkle with thyme. Broil until the tomatoes are golden brown, about 2 minutes.

6. Top each bruschetta with chopped arugula and drizzle with balsamic vinegar.

LENTIL AND CORN SALAD WITH SWEET PEPPERS AND BASIL

THIS PRETTY SUMMER LENTIL AND BARLEY SALAD HAS A TERRIFIC CRUNCHY TEXTURE AND AN INTENSE BALSAMIC-GARLIC VINAIGRETTE.

YIELD: 4 SERVINGS

½ cup pearl barley
½ cup lentils
2 tablespoons coarse sea salt or
    kosher salt, plus additional to taste

For the vinaigrette
2 ½ tablespoons balsamic vinegar
1 ½ tablespoons freshly squeezed
    lemon juice
1 garlic clove, peeled
1 teaspoon coarse sea salt or
    kosher salt
5 tablespoons extra-virgin olive oil

4 ears corn, shucked
½ pound green beans, trimmed
    and cut into ½-inch pieces
    (about 2 cups)
1 red bell pepper, cut into thin
    ½-inch strips
1 yellow bell pepper, cut into thin
    ½-inch strips
2 scallions, green and white parts
    only, thinly sliced
⅓ cup packed fresh basil leaves
Freshly milled black pepper

1. In a large pot over high heat, bring 3 quarts of water to a boil. Add the barley and lentils and boil for 10 minutes. Add 2 tablespoons of salt and boil until al dente, about 10 more minutes.

2. Meanwhile, prepare the vinaigrette: In a small bowl, whisk together the vinegar and lemon juice. Use a garlic press to crush the garlic into the bowl and stir in the salt. Let this mixture marinate for 5 minutes, then whisk in the oil.

3. Add the corn and green beans to the pot and boil until the green beans are crisp-tender, about 3 to 4 minutes. Drain the contents of the pot in a colander and cool under cold running water. Transfer the corn to a cutting board and cut off the kernels.

4. In a serving bowl, combine the barley, lentils, beans, corn kernels, peppers, and scallions and toss with the vinaigrette. Tear the basil into bite-sized pieces and toss them into the salad. Season with additional salt and pepper.

PEELING PEPPERS

Quartering peppers and then removing their skins with a vegetable peeler is something everyone should try. It makes peppers more digestible (this is why they're often grilled and skinned in many Italian dishes), and what you're left with is something that's sweet, tender, and still crispy. Sautéed peeled peppers are incredible—they just melt into a delicious sauce.

MENU 7

•

CRACKED WHEAT

•

TEMPEH
RATATOUILLE

MARKET LIST

FRESH PRODUCE
2 pints cherry tomatoes
1 pound summer squash
1 pound eggplant
   (1 medium)
1 large yellow or
   red bell pepper
1 large onion
Garlic
Basil
Parsley
1 lemon

DAIRY AND SOY
Unsalted butter
4 ounces Parmesan
   cheese (optional)
2 (8-ounce) packages soy
   tempeh

PANTRY
Extra-virgin olive oil
8 ounces bulgur wheat
Crushed red pepper
   flakes
Coarse sea salt or
   kosher salt

EQUIPMENT
Medium saucepan
   with lid
Large skillet with lid
Box grater (if using
   Parmesan)
Citrus juicer

MENU 7 GAME PLAN
1. Prepare the bulgur.
2. Prepare the ratatouille.
3. Fluff the bulgur and serve
   with ratatouille.

CRACKED WHEAT

YIELD: 4 TO 6 SERVINGS

1 cup medium or coarse bulgur wheat
½ teaspoon coarse sea salt or kosher salt
1 tablespoon unsalted butter

1. In a medium saucepan, combine 1¼ cups water, the salt, and butter. Bring to a boil over high heat. Stir in the bulgur, reduce the heat, and simmer, covered, for 30 seconds. Remove the pan from the heat, still covered, and set aside for 20 minutes.

2. Transfer the bulgur to a bowl and fluff with a fork.

BULGUR WHEAT is a traditional staple of the Middle East. Whole grain wheat is steamed, dried, and cracked. The lighter varieties made from golden durum wheat are my favorite. Toothsome medium and coarse grades are perfect for this menu, whereas a fine grade is preferable for tabbouleh (see page 33). If you can't find bulgur wheat, substitute couscous.

TEMPEH RATATOUILLE

TEMPEH GIVES THIS RATATOUILLE HEFT AND TURNS IT INTO A
MAIN COURSE. THE TEMPEH GETS INFUSED WITH ALL THE
GOOD FLAVORS OF THE VEGETABLES AND AROMATICS.

YIELD: 4 TO 6 SERVINGS

½ cup extra-virgin olive oil
2 (8 ounce) packages soy tempeh,
    cut into ½-inch cubes
1 large onion, diced (about 2 cups)
Coarse sea salt or kosher salt
3 garlic cloves, chopped
1 teaspoon crushed red pepper
    flakes
2 pints cherry tomatoes, halved
1 pound summer squash, cut into 1-inch cubes
1 pound eggplant (1 medium), cut into 1-inch cubes
1 large yellow or red bell pepper, halved, seeded,
    and cut into 1-inch pieces
¼ cup chopped fresh basil, plus additional
    for garnish
2 tablespoons chopped fresh flat-leaf parsley
Juice of 1 lemon
Grated Parmesan cheese garnish for (optional)

1. In a large skillet over high heat, warm the oil. Add the tempeh, onion, and 2 teaspoons of salt
and sauté for 5 minutes. Add the garlic and red pepper flakes and sauté for 1 minute more.

2. Add the tomatoes, squash, eggplant, bell pepper, basil, and 1 ½ cups of water, raise the heat,
and bring to a simmer. Cover and cook over high heat for 15 minutes. Stir in the parsley and
lemon juice and season with additional salt to taste.

3. Serve the ratatouille over cracked wheat, garnished with additional basil and Parmesan
cheese, if desired.

MENU 8

•

WHOLE GRAIN PASTA
WITH SALSA CRUDA

•

WHITE BEAN AND
ARUGULA SALAD WITH
LEMON DILL VINAIGRETTE

MARKET LIST

FRESH PRODUCE
3 bunches arugula
1 yellow bell pepper
2 pounds ripe tomatoes
Chives
Garlic
Basil
Flat-leaf parsley
Dill
2 lemons

DAIRY
4 ounces Parmesan
    cheese

PANTRY
Extra-virgin olive oil
Balsamic vinegar
12 ounces whole wheat
    fusilli or penne
1 (15-ounce) can
    white beans
Coarse sea salt or
    kosher salt
Black peppercorns

EQUIPMENT
Large pot
Wire whisk
Citrus juicer

MENU 8 GAME PLAN

1. Bring a large pot of water to a boil water for the tomatoes and pasta.
2. Whisk the lemon dill vinaigrette in a large bowl.
3. Prepare the yellow pepper and white beans for the salad and toss them with the vinaigrette. Set aside to marinate.
4. Wash and dry the arugula and refrigerate until ready to use.
5. Prepare the salsa cruda (reserve the water for the pasta).
6. Cook the pasta.
7. Chop the arugula and toss it with the white beans. Season with salt and pepper.
8. Toss the pasta with the salsa and herbs.
9. Serve the pasta and salad on separate plates. Accompany with a chunk of Parmesan for shaving.

WHOLE GRAIN PASTA WITH SALSA CRUDA

SALSA CRUDA IS AN UNCOOKED PASTA SAUCE THAT'S IDEAL
FOR MAKING IN THE SUMMER WHEN FRESH TOMATOES AND
HERBS ARE AT THEIR PEAK. YOU CAN ALSO TRY MAKING THE
SALSA WITH ASSORTED VARIETIES OF CHERRY TOMATOES.
SIMPLY HALVE OR QUARTER THEM AND ELIMINATE THE
BLANCHING AND PEELING STEP.

YIELD: 4 SERVINGS

2 pounds ripe tomatoes, cored and
    scored with a small "X" at the rounded end
2 tablespoons coarse sea salt or
    kosher salt, plus additional to taste
¾ pound whole wheat fusilli or penne
⅓ cup extra-virgin olive oil
¼ cup roughly chopped fresh
    flat-leaf parsley
6 to 8 fresh basil leaves, torn
2 tablespoons minced chives
2 tablespoons balsamic vinegar
2 garlic cloves, minced
Freshly milled black pepper
Parmesan cheese for serving

1. Fill a large pot with water, cover and bring to a boil. Add the 2 tablespoons of salt. Drop the tomatoes into the water and blanch for 30 seconds. Remove the tomatoes with a slotted spoon and peel them under cool running water. Slice each tomato in half along the equator, remove the seeds with your fingers, and discard. Roughly chop the tomato flesh and place it in a large serving bowl.

2. Return the water to a boil. Stir in the pasta and cook until al dente, about 10 minutes.

3. Meanwhile, add the oil, parsley, basil, chives, vinegar, and garlic to the tomatoes.

4. Drain the pasta and transfer immediately to the bowl with the tomato mixture. Toss well and season with salt and pepper. Serve immediately.

WHITE BEAN AND ARUGULA SALAD WITH LEMON DILL VINAIGRETTE

THIS SUBSTANTIAL SALAD, SERVED SIMPLY WITH GOOD CRUSTY BREAD, IS GREAT FOR LUNCH. USE A VEGETABLE PEELER TO SHAVE THE PARMESAN CHEESE.

YIELD: 4 SERVINGS

⅓ cup extra-virgin olive oil

3 tablespoons freshly squeezed lemon juice

1 tablespoon minced fresh dill

1 small garlic clove, finely chopped

Coarse sea salt or kosher salt and
   freshly milled black pepper

3 bunches arugula, trimmed and roughly
   chopped (6 to 7 cups)

1 (15-ounce) can white beans, such as cannellini
   or Great Northern, drained

1 yellow bell pepper, halved, seeded and thinly
   sliced

Shaved Parmesan cheese for garnish

1. In a large bowl, whisk together the oil, lemon juice, dill, garlic, and salt and pepper. Add the arugula, beans, and yellow pepper and toss to combine.

2. Garnish the salad with shaved Parmesan cheese and serve.

FLAVORFUL SALADS

Whether you are making a leafy green salad or grain, bean, or pasta salad, make sure all your ingredients are drained thoroughly of surface water. Otherwise, the dressing will be diluted and the flavor and texture of the finished dish will be diminished.

MENU 9

•

ASIAN CUCUMBER SALAD

•

THAI-STYLE TOFU AND VEGETABLES IN SPICY COCONUT BROTH WITH JASMINE RICE

MARKET LIST

FRESH PRODUCE

2 medium tomatoes
½ pound snow peas
2 pounds Asian or
   Kirby cucumbers
2 serrano chiles
1 fresh red chile pepper
1 head Napa cabbage
2 medium carrots
1 scallion
½ pound shallots
Ginger
Garlic
¼ pound fresh shiitake or
   white mushrooms
Basil
1 lemon
1 lime

SOY

1 pound firm tofu

PANTRY

Neutral oil, such as
   grapeseed, canola or
   sunflower
Toasted sesame oil
Rice vinegar
Soy sauce
Crushed red pepper
   flakes (if not using fresh
   red chile)
Ground turmeric
1 (14-ounce) can
   coconut milk
Sugar
Coarse sea salt or
   kosher salt
8 ounces white jasmine
   rice
2 (4-inch) pieces dried
   wakame seaweed

EQUIPMENT

Large saucepan
Benriner or mandoline
   (optional)
Small pot with lid
   (for cooking the rice)
Colander
Wire whisk
Citrus juicer

MENU 9 GAME PLAN

1. Prepare the cucumber
   salad through step 3.
2. Cook the rice.
3. Prepare the tofu and
   vegetables through step
   1.
4. Finish the cucumber
   salad and refrigerate.
5. Finish the tofu and
   vegetables and slice
   the lime.
6. Serve the stew in deep
   bowls with jasmine rice
   and lime wedges. Serve
   the cucumber salad on
   the side in small dishes.

ASIAN CUCUMBER SALAD

THIS SWEET-AND-SPICY CUCUMBER SALAD IS BEST MADE
WITH ASIAN OR KIRBY CUCUMBERS, WHICH HAVE SMALL
SEEDS AND THIN, EDIBLE SKINS. FOR MAXIMUM SPEED AND
EASE, USE A BENRINER OR MANDOLINE (SEE PAGE 10) TO
SLICE THE CUCUMBERS AND JULIENNE THE CARROTS.

YIELD: 4 SERVINGS

2 (4-inch) pieces dried wakame seaweed

2 pounds Asian or Kirby cucumbers,
     unpeeled, very thinly sliced

1 medium carrot, peeled and cut into
     matchsticks or coarsely shredded

1 tablespoon coarse sea salt or
     kosher salt

2 tablespoons rice vinegar

2 tablespoons freshly squeezed
     lemon juice

1 teaspoon sugar, preferably organic
     washed cane sugar (see page 8)

2 teaspoons toasted sesame oil

1 fresh red chile, with seeds, thinly sliced,
     or ½ teaspoon crushed red pepper flakes

1. In a small bowl soak the wakame in 2 cups of water and set aside until it is soft, about 15 minutes.

2. Place a colander inside a bowl. Put the cucumber and carrot in the colander and toss with the salt. Refrigerate for 15 minutes.

3. Combine the vinegar, lemon juice, and sugar in a small bowl, and whisk until the sugar dissolves. Stir in the sesame oil and chile.

4. Squeeze out excess moisture from the cucumbers and carrots and transfer them to a salad bowl.

5. Drain the wakame and trim off any tough rib portions. Chop the wakame into bite-size pieces and add it to the salad along with the vinaigrette. Toss well and serve immediately, or chill for 15 minutes beforehand.

THAI-STYLE TOFU AND VEGETABLES IN SPICY COCONUT BROTH WITH JASMINE RICE

THIS CLASSIC SPICY STEW IS GREAT IN THE SUMMER WHEN THE MARKETS ARE OVERFLOWING WITH FRESH TOMATOES AND BASIL, BUT IT'S ALSO HEARTY ENOUGH SO THAT YOU CAN MAKE IT YEAR-ROUND. JUST SUBSTITUTE GREEN BEANS OR BROCCOLI FOR THE SNOW PEAS, AND CANNED TOMATOES FOR THE FRESH.

YIELD: 4 SERVINGS

1 cup thinly sliced shallots (about 4 large shallots)

2 tablespoons neutral oil, such as grapeseed, canola, or sunflower

2 serrano chiles, with seeds, thinly sliced

1 (1-inch) piece fresh ginger peeled and cut into matchsticks

1 garlic clove, chopped

1 teaspoon ground turmeric

1½ cups Napa cabbage, cut into ½-inch-wide strips

1 medium carrot, peeled and thinly sliced on the bias

1 cup sliced fresh shiitake or white mushroom caps

1 (14-ounce) can coconut milk

1 pound firm tofu, drained and cut into 1-inch cubes

2 tablespoons soy sauce

2 teaspoons coarse sea salt or kosher salt

2 medium tomatoes, cored and cut into wedges

1 cup snow peas, strings removed, cut in half crosswise

½ cup fresh basil leaves, torn into pieces

1 scallion, green part cut into 1-inch lengths, white part thinly sliced

1½ cups jasmine rice, cooked according to the package directions (see page 231)

1 lime, cut into wedges, for serving

1. In a large saucepan over high heat, combine the shallots and oil and sauté for 2 minutes. Reduce the heat to medium, add the chiles, ginger, garlic, and turmeric, and sauté for 1 minute more. Add the cabbage, carrot, and mushrooms and sauté for 2 more minutes, until the vegetables soften.

2. Pour in the coconut milk and 1 cup of water and bring the mixture to a boil. Add the tofu, soy sauce, and salt and simmer, uncovered, for 5 minutes. Add the tomatoes and snow peas and simmer for 3 more minutes. Add the basil and scallion and simmer for 1 minute more.

3. Serve with jasmine rice and lime wedges.

MENU 10

•

SPICY SUMMER BEAN AND
CHICKPEA SALAD WITH
HARISSA VINAIGRETTE

•

FRESH CORN POLENTA
WITH SAUTÉED CHERRY
TOMATOES

MARKET LIST

FRESH PRODUCE
1 large or 2 medium ears
   fresh corn
2 pints cherry tomatoes
½ pound green beans
½ pound yellow wax beans
Mixed fresh herbs,
   such as oregano, basil,
   tarragon, or parsley
1 small red onion
Garlic
2 lemons

DAIRY
Unsalted butter
4 ounces Parmesan
   cheese

PANTRY
Extra-virgin olive oil
Crushed red pepper
   flakes
Cumin seeds
Caraway seeds
Fennel seeds
Cayenne pepper
Coarse sea salt or
   kosher salt
Black peppercorns
½ pound fine or medium
   yellow corn grits
1 (15-ounce) can
   chickpeas

EQUIPMENT
Large skillet
6- to 8-quart pot
Medium saucepan with lid
Spice mill or mortar and
   pestle
Box grater

MENU 10 GAME PLAN
1. Fill large pot two-thirds
   full with water and place
   over high heat.
2. Make the polenta through
   step 2.
3. Prepare the vegetables
   for the salad.
4. Make the salad.
5. Finish the polenta.

SPICY SUMMER BEAN AND CHICKPEA SALAD WITH HARISSA VINAIGRETTE

HARISSA IS A VIBRANT, FIERY HOT CONDIMENT FROM NORTH AFRICA. THE TRADITIONAL MIXTURE OF LIGHTLY TOASTED FRESH GROUND SPICES AND GARLIC FORM THE BASE OF THIS ZESTY VINAIGRETTE. IF WAX BEANS ARE UNAVAILABLE USE ALL GREEN BEANS.

YIELD: 4 SERVINGS

Coarse sea salt or kosher salt
½ pound yellow wax beans, trimmed
½ pound green beans, trimmed
½ small red onion, sliced paper thin
1 (15-ounce) can chickpeas, drained
1 plump clove garlic, peeled
2 teaspoons cumin seeds
1 teaspoon caraway or fennel seeds
1 teaspoon cayenne pepper
3 tablespoons lemon juice
4 tablespoons extra-virgin olive oil

1. Bring a large pot of water to a boil. Add 1 tablespoon salt. When the water resumes a boil add the wax and green beans and boil for 2 to 3 minutes until crisp tender. Drain the beans and refresh under cold running water. Drain and spread on a clean cotton towel.

2. Peel the garlic and crush it with the side of a heavy knife. Sprinkle with a little salt and set aside for 5 minutes.

3. Meanwhile, toast the cumin and caraway seeds in a small skillet over medium heat for 1 minute until they are fragrant and turn a shade darker. Transfer the spices to a spice mill or mortar and pestle and grind them to a powder.

4. Chop and smear the garlic with the side of your knife until it forms a paste. Transfer the paste to a large serving bowl and add the lemon juice.

5. Stir the ground spices into the lemon juice. Whisk in the olive oil.

6. Add the sliced onion, chickpeas, and cooked beans to the bowl and toss to combine. Season with salt and serve immediately.

FRESH CORN POLENTA WITH SAUTÉED CHERRY TOMATOES

THE FASTEST WAY TO MAKE A TOMATO SAUCE IS TO USE CHERRY TOMATOES. THERE'S NO PEELING OR CHOPPING— YOU JUST THROW THEM IN. TRY MIXING DIFFERENT VARIETIES, SUCH AS YELLOW PEAR, ORANGE SUNBURST, AND COMMON RED ONES. I ALWAYS MAKE POLENTA WITH CORN GRITS, NEVER FROM CORNMEAL, WHICH GOES RANCID QUICKLY. YOU CAN FURTHER ENHANCE THIS MEAL BY TOPPING EACH SERVING OF POLENTA WITH A FRIED EGG.

YIELD: 4 SERVINGS

For the polenta

2 tablespoons unsalted butter

1 teaspoon coarse sea salt or
    kosher salt

1 cup coarsely ground polenta or
    corn grits

1 large or 2 medium ears fresh corn, kernels
    scraped off the cob (1 cup)

For the cherry tomatoes

2 pints cherry tomatoes

¼ cup extra-virgin olive oil

2 garlic cloves, minced

½ teaspoon crushed red pepper flakes

¼ cup chopped mixed fresh herbs, such as
    oregano, basil, tarragon, and parsley

Coarse sea salt or kosher salt and freshly
    milled black pepper

Grated Parmesan cheese for garnish

1. Preheat the oven to 200°F.

2. To prepare the polenta, in a medium saucepan over high heat, bring 3 cups of water to a boil, and add the butter and salt. Stir in the grits and corn and continue to stir until the water returns to a boil. Reduce the heat and simmer, uncovered, for 5 to 7 minutes, stirring occasionally, until the polenta is thick and smooth. Cover and transfer to the oven to keep warm.

3. To prepare the tomatoes, place a large skillet (it should be large enough to hold the tomatoes in a single layer) over high heat. Put the tomatoes, oil, garlic and red pepper flakes in the pan and sauté until the tomatoes soften and begin to exude their juice, about 3 to 4 minutes. Stir in the herbs and sauté for 2 more minutes. Season with salt and pepper.

4. Divide the polenta among 4 shallow soup plates and spoon the tomatoes on top. Serve sprinkled with Parmesan.

MENU 11

•

PITA PIZZA WITH GREEN OLIVES, MONTEREY JACK, AND CHOPPED SALAD

•

PAN-SEARED SUMMER SQUASH WITH GARLIC AND MINT

MARKET LIST

FRESH PRODUCE
3 hearts of romaine lettuce
4 medium Kirby cucumbers
2 medium tomatoes
1 ripe avocado
2 pounds summer squash
2 jalapeño peppers
1 small red onion
Garlic
Basil
Mint
1 lemon

DAIRY
8 ounces Monterey Jack cheese
4 ounces Parmesan cheese

PANTRY
Extra-virgin olive oil
Balsamic vinegar
Crushed red pepper flakes
½ cup green olives
Coarse sea salt or kosher salt
Black peppercorns
4 (7-inch) rounds of pocket-less pita bread

EQUIPMENT
Large heavy skillet, griddle, or grill pan
Pizza stone or heavy 11 x 17-inch rimmed baking sheet
Box grater
Citrus juicer

MENU 11 GAME PLAN
1. Preheat the oven to 450°F.
2. Prepare the squash salad.
3. Prepare the vegetables for the chopped salad.
4. Prepare the vinaigrette.
5. Make the pizzas.
6. Finish the salad and mound it on the pizzas. Shave some Parmesan cheese over the pizzas and serve immediately, accompanied by the squash.

PITA PIZZA WITH GREEN OLIVES, MONTEREY JACK, AND CHOPPED SALAD

POCKETLESS PITA BREAD MAKES A CONVENIENT PIZZA BASE.
YOU COULD ALSO USE ANY OTHER TENDER, CHEWY
FLATBREAD, SUCH AS LAVASH.

YIELD: 4 SERVINGS

For the chopped salad
1 garlic clove, peeled and halved
2 tablespoons balsamic vinegar
1 small red onion, halved and very thinly sliced
¼ cup extra-virgin olive oil
Coarse sea salt or kosher salt and
    freshly milled black pepper
3 hearts of romaine, coarsely chopped
    (about 8 cups)
4 medium Kirby cucumbers, quartered lengthwise
    and cut into bite-sized pieces
2 medium tomatoes, cored, seeded, and diced
    (about 1 cup)
1 ripe avocado, diced
5 fresh basil leaves, torn into pieces
8 to 10 fresh mint leaves, torn into pieces

For the pizzas
4 (7-inch) rounds of pocketless pita bread
8 ounces Monterey Jack cheese, coarsely grated
½ cup pitted and roughly chopped green olives
2 jalapeño peppers, minced, or 1 teaspoon
    crushed red pepper flakes
Freshly milled black pepper
Shaved Parmesan cheese for garnish

1. Place a pizza stone or an inverted rimmed baking sheet in the upper third of the oven and preheat the oven to 450°F.

2. To prepare the salad, vigorously rub the inside of a large bowl with the garlic. Add

vinegar and red onion and set aside for 5 minutes. Whisk in the oil and season with salt and pepper. Add the lettuce, cucumber, tomato, avocado, basil, and mint and toss well.

3. Bake the pitas, in batches if necessary, on the heated pizza stone or pan for 3 minutes.

4. In a small bowl, combine the cheese, olives, and jalapeños. Divide this mixture among the 4 pitas.

5. Return the pitas to the oven, 2 at a time, and bake until the cheese is bubbling and lightly browned, about 5 minutes.

6. Mound the salad on top of the pizzas, sprinkle with Parmesan cheese, and serve.

PAN-SEARED SUMMER SQUASH WITH GARLIC AND MINT

PAN SEARING THE SQUASH CARAMELIZES IT AND PRODUCES A NICE CRUST. THE SUGARS BECOME CONCENTRATED AND THE JUICES ARE LOCKED IN. YOU CAN USE THE SAME TECHNIQUE WITH EGGPLANT SLICES AND ONION RINGS.

YIELD: 4 SERVINGS

2 pounds summer squash, sliced ½-inch-thick
2 tablespoons freshly squeezed lemon juice
2 tablespoons fresh mint, torn into pieces
2 garlic cloves, finely chopped
1 teaspoon coarse sea salt or kosher
    salt, plus additional to taste
½ teaspoon crushed red pepper flakes
3 tablespoons extra-virgin olive oil
Freshly milled black pepper

1. Warm a large heavy skillet, griddle, or grill pan over medium heat. Arrange the squash in a single layer and sear until speckled with brown and beginning to blacken, about 5 minutes more. Flip the squash and cook for 4 to 5 minutes more. Repeat with remaining squash.

2. In a serving bowl, combine the lemon juice, mint, garlic, salt, and red pepper flakes and let marinate for 5 minutes. Whisk in the oil.

3. Transfer the seared squash to the bowl, toss to coat with the dressing, and let rest for about 5 minutes. Season with additional salt and pepper and serve.

MENU 12

•

EDAMAME

•

CHILLED SOBA NOODLES IN DASHI WITH TOFU AND SHREDDED ROMAINE

MARKET LIST

FRESH PRODUCE
1 head romaine lettuce
1 pound edamame
1 medium daikon or
    1 bunch red radish
1 medium carrot
Scallions
Ginger

SOY
1 pound soft tofu

PANTRY
4 ounces mirin
Rice vinegar
8 ounces soy sauce
12 ounces soba noodles
1 (3- to 4-inch) strip
    kombu seaweed
1 sheet sushi nori
Coarse sea salt or
    kosher salt

EQUIPMENT
Large pot
Large saucepan
Small saucepan
Benriner or mandoline
    (optional)
Box grater
Kitchen shears

MENU 12 GAME PLAN
1. Boil water in separate
   pots for the edamame
   and the soba.
2. Boil, drain, and chill
   the soba.
3. Prepare the edamame.
4. Make the dashi.
5. Prepare the garnishes.
6. Serve the soba, dashi,
   and garnishes in large
   bowls, accompanied by
   the edamame.

EDAMAME

IF YOU CAN'T FIND NICE, PLUMP EDAMAME (FRESH
SOYBEANS) IN YOUR LOCAL FARMER'S MARKET, LOOK FOR
ORGANIC EDAMAME IN THE FROZEN-FOOD SECTION OF YOUR
SUPERMARKET OR HEALTH FOOD STORE, AND BOIL OR
STEAM THEM ACCORDING TO THE PACKAGE DIRECTIONS.

YIELD: **4** SERVINGS

1 pound fresh edamame
1 tablespoon coarse sea salt or kosher salt,
  plus additional for sprinkling

1. Fill a large saucepan with water and bring to a boil. Add the edamame and salt and boil for 2 minutes. Drain and cool under cold running water.

2. Spread the edamame on a cloth towel to absorb excess moisture. Transfer to small bowls, sprinkle with additional salt, and serve.

CHILLED SOBA NOODLES IN DASHI WITH TOFU AND SHREDDED ROMAINE

HERE'S ANOTHER EXAMPLE OF HOW LETTUCE CAN BE ENJOYED IN AN UNTRADITIONAL WAY. ADDED AS A GARNISH TO THIS CHILLED SUMMER SOUP, IT BECOMES A REFRESHING COUNTERPOINT TO THE SOFT NOODLES AND TOFU. CHILLED SOBA IS ONE OF MY FAVORITE MEALS TO BEAT THE HEAT OF SUMMER. HERE I'VE REVAMPED A FAVORITE RECIPE FROM MY FIRST BOOK, *THE MODERN VEGETARIAN KITCHEN*. THE DISH IS READY IN LESS THAN HALF THE TIME OF THE ORIGINAL, AND IS JUST AS REFRESHING.

YIELD: 4 SERVINGS

12 ounces soba noodles
1 (3- to 4-inch strip) of kombu
    seaweed, broken in half
½ cup soy sauce
⅓ cup mirin (see page 135)
3 tablespoons rice vinegar
1 tablespoon finely grated fresh ginger
3 cups shredded romaine lettuce
1 pound soft tofu, drained and
    patted dry
1 cup matchsticks or coarsely shredded
    daikon or red radish
1 cup matchsticks or coarsely shredded carrot
1 scallion, trimmed and thinly sliced
Ice cubes for serving (optional)
1 sheet sushi nori, cut into strips
    with kitchen shears

1. Fill a large pot two-thirds full with water and bring to a boil. Add the soba noodles and cook until al dente, about 8 minutes. Drain and chill under cold running water. Drain again and divide among 4 large serving bowls.

2. To prepare the dashi, in a small saucepan over medium heat, combine 1 cup of water with the kombu and simmer gently for 1 minute. Discard the kombu or save for another use such as a soup or stew.

3. In a medium bowl, combine 1 ½ cups of ice water with the dashi, soy sauce, mirin, vinegar, and ginger.

4. In a large bowl, toss together the lettuce, tofu, daikon, carrot, and scallion.

5. Ladle the dashi mixture over the noodles and top with tofu and vegetables. Sprinkle the bowls with nori strips and serve immediately, with ice cubes, if desired.

MIRIN is sweet Japanese rice wine. I use it to mellow out salty flavors or naturally acidic dishes, such as tomato sauces. It also partners well with the strong flavors of soy sauce, ginger, garlic, and sesame oil. You can find good quality mirin at most health food stores.

SUMMER

Roasted Peaches with Raspberry Sauce
and Whipped Greek-Style Yogurt with Cinnamon

Lemon-Ricotta Soufflé with Blueberries

Roasted Apricots in Reisling with
Black Pepper

Blueberry-Nectarine Crisp

Summer Fruit Salad in Herbed Wine Syrup

Blueberries in Muscat Wine with
Vanilla Ice Cream

Strawberries in Champagne

Watermelon with Fleur de Sel

Roasted Fresh Figs with Raspberries

Warm Summer Berries with Whipped Crème Fraîche

DESSERTS

ROASTED PEACHES WITH RASPBERRY SAUCE AND WHIPPED GREEK-STYLE YOGURT WITH CINNAMON

THIS DESSERT USES THE SAME PEACH-AND-RASPBERRY FLAVOR COMBINATION AS PEACH MELBA, BUT SUBSTITUTES THICK GREEK YOGURT FOR THE VANILLA ICE CREAM.

YIELD: 4 SERVINGS

For the peaches

1 tablespoon unsalted butter at room
   temperature
2 tablespoons brown sugar, such as
   Demerara (see page 8)
½ teaspoon pure vanilla extract
4 ripe peaches, halved and pitted

For the raspberry sauce

1 pint raspberries
Sugar, preferably organic washed cane
   sugar (see page 8), to taste

For the yogurt

1 cup labneh yogurt
¼ teaspoon pure vanilla extract
2 tablespoons sugar, preferably organic
   washed cane sugar (see page 8)
½ cinnamon stick, freshly ground in a spice
   mill, or ½ teaspoon ground cinnamon

1. Set racks on the top and bottom positions of the oven and preheat to 425°F.

2. To prepare the peaches, butter a 6-cup baking dish and sprinkle it evenly with the sugar and vanilla extract. Arrange the peach halves, cut side down, in the pan and roast on the bottom shelf of the oven until they begin to caramelize, about 7 to 8 minutes. Turn over the peaches and transfer the pan to the top shelf of the oven. Roast until the fruit is tender, about 3 to 4 more minutes.

3. To prepare the sauce, puree the raspberries in a blender or food processor. Set a sieve over a small bowl and strain the berries through it, pressing down with a rubber spatula. Scrape any sauce clinging to the underside of the sieve into the bowl. Discard the seeds. Whisk in sugar to taste.

4. To prepare the yogurt, combine the labneh, vanilla, and sugar in a chilled bowl and whip until the yogurt holds soft peaks.

5. Spoon 2 to 3 tablespoons of raspberry sauce in each of 4 shallow bowls. Top with 2 peach halves and a dollop of whipped yogurt. Dust each serving with freshly ground cinnamon to taste and serve. Pass the remaining sauce on the side.

LABNEH is a Middle Eastern yogurt with a very thick, sour-creamy texture. If you want to make your own, drain plain whole-milk yogurt in a cheesecloth-lined strainer overnight in the fridge. Or you can simply substitute sour cream.

LEMON-RICOTTA SOUFFLÉ
WITH BLUEBERRIES

THIS WARM, PUFFY DESSERT CAN BE MADE WITH RASPBERRIES
OR BLACKBERRIES WITH EQUALLY GREAT RESULTS.

YIELD: 6 TO 8 SERVINGS

½ cup sugar, preferably organic washed
　　cane sugar (see page 8)
6 large eggs
Grated zest of 1 lemon
1 pound whole-milk ricotta cheese
1 pint blueberries

1. Set a rack in the lower third of the oven and preheat to 375°F. Butter a 9-inch pie plate or baking dish. Set aside 1 tablespoon of the sugar.

2. In a medium bowl, whisk together the eggs, remaining 7 tablespoons of sugar, and lemon zest. Add the ricotta and whisk until smooth.

3. Pour the mixture into the pie plate and bake for 15 minutes. Top with the blueberries, sprinkle with the remaining tablespoon of sugar, and bake until just set, about 15 minutes more. Serve warm or chilled.

ROASTED APRICOTS IN RIESLING WITH BLACK PEPPER

ROASTING APRICOTS, EVEN FOR JUST A FEW MINUTES
AS I SUGGEST HERE, REALLY BRINGS OUT THEIR SWEET,
SYRUPY FLAVOR.

YIELD: 4 SERVINGS

1 pound apricots, halved and pitted
2 to 3 tablespoons sugar,
    preferably organic washed cane sugar
    (see page 8)
Pinch of freshly milled black
    pepper
½ cup late harvest Riesling or other
    dessert wine

1. Set a rack in the upper third of the oven and preheat to 425°F.

2. Arrange the apricot halves, cut side up, on a 9-inch pie plate or baking dish. Sprinkle them evenly with the sugar and pepper.

3. In a medium saucepan over high heat, bring the wine to a simmer.

4. Gently pour the wine around the fruit without disturbing the sugar and pepper. Roast in the oven until the apricots begin to caramelize, about 7 minutes. Turn the fruit over and roast until the apricots are tender, but not falling apart, about 2 to 3 more minutes.

BLUEBERRY-NECTARINE CRISP

YOU CAN USE THIS BASIC CRISP RECIPE WITH A
VARIETY OF SEASONAL FRUITS. TRY PEARS OR
APPLES IN FALL AND WINTER, AND RHUBARB AND
STRAWBERRIES IN SPRING.

YIELD: 6 SERVINGS

4 ripe nectarines, halved, pitted, and cut
    into ½-inch slices
1 pint blueberries
¾ cup brown sugar, preferably
    Demerara (see page 8)
Finely grated zest of ½ lemon
1 cup unbleached all-purpose flour
½ cup unsalted butter (1 stick) at room
    temperature
½ cup sugar, preferably organic washed cane
    sugar (see page 8)
½ cup sliced almonds
Vanilla ice cream for serving

1. Set a rack in the bottom third of the oven and preheat to 425°F.

2. In a medium bowl, toss the nectarines with the blueberries, brown sugar, and lemon zest.

3. In another medium bowl, combine the flour, butter, and sugar and with your fingers, rub the butter into the dry ingredients until the flour has absorbed most of it. Stir in the almonds.

4. Transfer the fruit mixture to a large ovenproof skillet. Spread the flour mixture over the fruit. Place the skillet over high heat and cook until the fruit begins to bubble. Transfer the pan to the oven and bake until the topping is golden brown and the fruit is bubbling and tender, about 20 minutes.

5. Allow the crisp to cool slightly and serve with ice cream.

SUMMER FRUIT SALAD IN HERBED WINE SYRUP

USE WHATEVER PERFECTLY RIPE FRUIT YOU FIND IN THE FARMER'S MARKET FOR THIS RECIPE.

YIELD: 4 SERVINGS

1 bottle dry white wine
½ cup mild honey
1 sprig fresh rosemary
1 (2-inch) stick cinnamon
1 vanilla bean, halved lengthwise, pulp scraped with a knife
2 pounds assorted ripe fruits, such as nectarines, peaches, apricots, figs, and cherries, pitted and sliced

1. In a medium saucepan over high heat, combine the wine, honey, rosemary, cinnamon stick, and vanilla pod and pulp. Bring the mixture to a boil and cook, uncovered, until it has reduced by two thirds and is syrupy, 15 to 20 minutes.

2. Put the fruits in a serving bowl, strain the wine syrup over them, and refrigerate until cold.

BLUEBERRIES IN MUSCAT WINE WITH VANILLA ICE CREAM

FROM MID JULY TO EARLY SEPTEMBER, BLUEBERRIES TAKE CENTER STAGE IN ALL KINDS OF DESSERTS. SINCE THE BERRIES REQUIRE NEITHER PEELING NOR PITTING, THEY ARE ONE OF NATURE'S TRUE CONVENIENCE FOODS.

YIELD: 4 SERVINGS

1 pint blueberries
1 cup Muscat Beaumes-de-Venise or any flavorful dessert wine
Vanilla ice cream for serving
Mint leaves for garnish

Divide the berries among 4 small bowls. Dowse each serving with wine and serve with a scoop of vanilla ice cream and a few torn mint leaves.

STRAWBERRIES IN CHAMPAGNE

THESE LUSCIOUS STRAWBERRIES WILL KEEP UP TO 3 DAYS IN THE REFRIGERATOR. THEY ARE A GREAT WAY TO DRESS UP POUND CAKE, CHOCOLATE CAKE, OR SHORTCAKE.

YIELD: 4 SERVINGS

¾ cup Champagne or another
    sparkling wine
3 tablespoons sugar, preferably organic washed
    cane sugar (see page 8)
1 pint strawberries, sliced
2 teaspoons finely grated orange or lemon zest
Vanilla, strawberry, or peach ice cream
    for serving
Fresh mint sprigs for garnish

1. In a large bowl, whisk together the champagne and sugar to taste until the sugar dissolves.

2. Stir in the berries and zest. Refrigerate for 30 minutes or more.

3. Serve with ice cream and mint.

WATERMELON WITH FLEUR DE SEL

THE SIMPLEST AND BEST DESSERT I KNOW.

YIELD: 4 SERVINGS

4 slices chilled watermelon
Fleur de sel

Sprinkle the melon lightly with salt and serve.

ROASTED FRESH FIGS
WITH RASPBERRIES

FRESH FIGS AND RASPBERRIES—WHAT COULD BE
MORE LUXURIOUS? AS THE FRUIT COOKS, THE
RASPBERRIES BURST AND RELEASE THEIR JUICES TO FORM A
DELECTABLE RUBY SAUCE FOR THE BUTTERY FIGS.

YIELD: 4 SERVINGS

1 pint raspberries
12 ripe Mission figs, stems trimmed,
    scored with an "X" on top
¼ cup (½ stick) chilled unsalted
    butter, cut into 12 pieces
2 tablespoons brown sugar,
    preferably Demerara
    (see page 8)

1. Set a rack in the top shelf of the oven and preheat to 425°F.

2. In a large ovenproof skillet, arrange the raspberries in one layer and top with the figs.

3. Tuck a piece of butter into each fig and sprinkle the sugar over all.

4. Place the skillet over high heat and cook until the raspberries begin to break down, about 3 minutes.

5. Transfer the skillet to the oven and roast until the figs begin to brown around the edges, about 8 to 10 minutes.

WARM SUMMER BERRIES WITH WHIPPED CRÈME FRAÎCHE

ELEGANT, SUPERFAST, AND SO EASY TO PREPARE—WHO CAN
RESIST THIS QUINTESSENTIAL SUMMER DELIGHT! IF YOU
DON'T HAVE CRÈME FRAÎCHE ON HAND, SERVE WITH YOUR
FAVORITE STORE-BOUGHT ICE CREAM.

YIELD: 4 TO 6 SERVINGS

1 pint raspberries
1 pint blueberries
1 pint black raspberries
3 tablespoons sugar, preferably organic washed
   cane sugar (see page 8)
1 cup crème fraîche for serving

1. In a large skillet, combine the berries and sprinkle them evenly with sugar.

2. Place the pan over high heat and simmer until the berries exude their juice but still hold their shape, about 2 minutes.

3. In a chilled bowl, whisk the crème fraîche until soft peaks form. Serve the berries with the crème fraîche.

Reflection. . . . Energy falls—the world comes down slowly from dizzying heights. Round and firm ripens into middle age. Pointed peppers and squashes give way to rounded pumpkins and cabbages. Take stock: There are grapes to crush and olives to mill, nuts to gather, and mushrooms to dry. The tender pods of legumes condense into beans. Green tomatoes fall from their vines to be gathered sour, or to shrivel and rot. The long harvest begins. We put food

AUTUMN

by and conserve. Our dishes mellow. Onions and garlic cure in the rafters. The burst of berries is now a sweet memory, like a summer fling. Royal stone fruits—apricot, peaches, and plums—give way to proletarian apples and pears.

AUTUMN

1. Wild Mushroom Fricassee over Farro
   Warm Mesclun Salad with Sherry Vinaigrette and Five-Minute Eggs

2. Radish, Orange, and Avocado Salad
   Black Bean Tostadas with Cherry Tomato Salsa

3. Romaine Salad with Sun-Dried Tomatoes and Lemon-Parmesan Dressing
   Wehani and Wild Rice Stew with Cremini Mushrooms, Winter Squash, and Kale

4. Red Lentil and Sweet Potato Curry with Warm Pita Bread
   Spicy Red Cabbage with Cumin Seeds and Tomatoes

5. Barley Risotto with Golden Beets, Swiss Chard, and Goat Cheese
   Fennel-Cabbage Slaw with Raisins and Apple

6. Pasta with Spicy Cauliflower, Chickpeas, and Cherry Tomatoes
   Pan-Grilled Radicchio Salad with Honey-Balsamic Glaze

7. Pumpkin, Pear, and Fennel Soup
   Quinoa with Brussels Sprouts, Tempeh, and Toasted Almonds

8. Giant Arepas with Aged Gouda
   Braised Pinto Beans with Delicata Squash, Red Wine, and Tomatoes

9. Roasted Winter Squash with Curry Butter and Apple Cider
   Stuffed Greens with Red Bean and Vegetables Ragout

10. Chipotle Roasted Potatoes
    Baked Eggs with Escarole, Onions, and Gruyère

11. Broccoli Salad with Ginger Vinaigrette
    Pad Thai

12. Bulgur and Buckwheat Pilaf
    Autumn Tempeh and Vegetable Stew

MENU 1

WILD MUSHROOM
FRICASSEE OVER FARRO

WARM MESCLUN
SALAD WITH SHERRY
VINAIGRETTE AND
FIVE-MINUTE EGGS

MARKET LIST

FRESH PRODUCE

1 pound mesclun greens
2 pounds mixed
    mushrooms, such as
    cremini, shiitake,
    chanterelle, and oyster
1 medium onion
2 large shallots
Garlic
Thyme
Rosemary
Flat-leaf parsley

DAIRY

Unsalted butter
4 large eggs
4 ounces hard grating
    cheese, such as
    Parmesan, Romano, or
    Grana Padano

PANTRY

Extra-virgin olive oil
Balsamic vinegar
Sherry vinegar
12 ounces farro, barley, or
    peeled wheat berries
All-purpose flour
Coarse sea salt or
    kosher salt
Black peppercorns
Dry red wine, such as
    Côtes du Rhône,
    Zinfandel, or Chianti

EQUIPMENT

Large heavy sauté pan
    with lid
Small skillet
Small saucepan with lid
Pressure cooker
11 x 17-inch heavy rimmed
    baking sheet
Box grater
Salad spinner
Tongs

MENU 1 GAME PLAN

1. Set a rimmed baking
   sheet on the middle shelf
   of the oven and preheat
   to 450°F.
2. Prepare the fricassee
   through step 7.
3. Prepare the salad through
   step 2.
4. Finish the fricassee.
5. Finish the salad and
   serve.
6. Serve the farro in deep
   soup plates with fricassee
   spooned on top.

WILD MUSHROOM FRICASSEE OVER FARRO

FARRO IS ANOTHER NAME FOR SPELT, AN ANCIENT, PROTEIN-RICH STRAIN OF WHEAT THAT CAN BE TOLERATED BY A LOT OF PEOPLE WHO ARE ALLERGIC TO MODERN WHEAT. IT'S A SEMIREFINED GRAIN—ONLY THE MOST OUTER HUSK IS REMOVED. THIS MAKES IT FASTER TO COOK AND EASIER TO CHEW AND DIGEST THAN WHOLE WHEAT BERRIES. LIKE RICE, FARRO WILL COOK ON THE STOVE TOP IN ABOUT 25 MINUTES, OR JUST 9 MINUTES IN A PRESSURE COOKER. YOU CAN SUBSTITUTE PEELED WHEAT BERRIES OR GRANO (POLISHED DURUM WHEAT) IF YOU LIKE, OR YOU CAN USE WHOLE WHEAT BERRIES OR SPELT BERRIES, BUT YOU HAVE TO SOAK THEM OVERNIGHT BEFORE COOKING. ALTERNATIVELY, YOU CAN SERVE THE FRICASSEE OVER PASTA, POLENTA, WHITE RICE, OR PEARL BARLEY.

YIELD: 4 SERVINGS

2 pounds mixed mushrooms, such as shiitake,
    chanterelle, cremini, and oyster, cleaned
3 tablespoons extra-virgin olive oil
1½ teaspoons coarse sea salt or
    kosher salt, plus additional to taste
Freshly milled black pepper
1½ cups farro, barley, or peeled wheat berries
2 tablespoons unsalted butter
1 medium onion, thinly sliced
2 teaspoons all-purpose flour
⅔ cup dry red wine
3 tablespoons finely chopped
    fresh flat-leaf parsley
2 tablespoons finely chopped fresh thyme
2 teaspoons finely chopped fresh rosemary
1 large garlic clove, finely chopped
Freshly grated hard grating cheese,
    such as Parmesan, Romano, or
    Grana Padano for garnish

1. To prepare the fricassee, place a rimmed baking sheet on the middle shelf of the oven and preheat to 450F°.

2. Cut the large mushrooms into 1-inch pieces, leaving small ones whole.

3. In a bowl, toss the mushrooms with 2 tablespoons of the oil, and season some with some salt and pepper. Carefully spread the mushrooms on the hot pan and roast for 15 minutes.

4. Meanwhile, prepare the farro. In a pressure cooker over high heat, bring 4 cups of water to a boil. Add the farro and 1 teaspoon of the salt and secure the lid. When the pot comes to full pressure, reduce the heat to medium-low and simmer for 9 minutes. Transfer the pot to the sink and run cold water over it to bring down the pressure. Test the farro for doneness and, if necessary, simmer, uncovered, for a few minutes more, until tender. Cover to keep warm.

5. Melt the butter in a large sauté pan over high heat. Add the onion and remaining ½ teaspoon of salt. Sauté until the onions begin to brown, about 5 minutes. Reduce the heat to low, cover the pan, and simmer for 5 minutes.

6. Transfer the roasted mushrooms to the pan with the onions. Add the flour and sauté, stirring, until the flour browns and begins to stick to the bottom of the pan, about 3 minutes.

7. Add the wine and ½ cup of water. Scrape up the brown bits from the bottom of the pan with a wooden spoon and bring to a boil. Reduce the heat to low and simmer until the sauce thickens, about 2 minutes.

8. Add the herbs and garlic to the pan and simmer for 1 minute. Season with salt and pepper. Serve over farro and sprinkle with grated Parmesan.

WARM MESCLUN SALAD WITH SHERRY VINAIGRETTE AND FIVE-MINUTE EGGS

THE FIVE-MINUTE EGG COMES WITH A SURPRISE BONUS. AS THE WHOLE EGG IS CUT, ITS YOLK FLOWS FORTH TO COAT THE SALAD GREENS, MAKING A RICH, CREAMY DRESSING.

YIELD: **4** SERVINGS

4 large eggs

1½ teaspoons coarse sea salt or kosher salt

1 small garlic clove, halved

1 pound mesclun or mixed baby greens

½ cup extra-virgin olive oil

¼ cup sherry vinegar

2 tablespoons balsamic vinegar

2 large shallots, peeled and chopped

2 teaspoons minced fresh thyme

Freshly milled black pepper

1. In a small saucepan over high heat, bring 1 quart of water to a boil. Add the eggs and 1 teaspoon of the salt, lower the heat, and simmer for 5 minutes. Transfer the eggs to a bowl of cold water to cool.

2. Rub the inside of a salad bowl with the garlic halves. Add the greens and set aside.

3. Place a small skillet over high heat and add the oil, sherry and balsamic vinegars, shallots, thyme, and remaining ½ teaspoon of salt. Cook for 1 minute. Turn off the heat and season with black pepper.

4. Pour the vinaigrette over the greens and toss well.

5. Crack the eggs all over and carefully peel under warm running water.

6. Divide the salad among 4 plates. Grind some black pepper over the salads and top each with a whole egg.

MENU 2

•

RADISH, ORANGE,
AND AVOCADO SALAD

•

BLACK BEAN
TOSTADAS WITH
CHERRY TOMATO
SALSA

MARKET LIST

FRESH PRODUCE

1 head romaine lettuce
1 pint cherry tomatoes
1 jalapeño pepper
1 large ripe Hass avocado
1 bunch red radishes
1 small onion
1 small red onion
Garlic
Cilantro
2 limes
1 lemon
2 large seedless oranges

DAIRY AND OTHER
PERISHABLES

1 (8-ounce) package
   seitan
16 ounces sour cream

PANTRY

Extra-virgin olive oil
Soy sauce
Cumin seeds
Dried oregano
Chipotle peppers in adobo
8 tostada shells
1 (15-ounce) can black
   beans
Coarse sea salt or
   kosher salt
Black peppercorns

EQUIPMENT

Large sauté pan
Citrus juicer

MENU 2 GAME PLAN

1. If you plan on making
   your own tostadas, bake
   them now. See the
   headnote on page 162.
2. Prepare the salsa and
   chill.
3. Prepare the salad and
   chill.
4. Sauté the black bean and
   seitan topping for the
   tostadas.
5. Shred the lettuce.
6. Serve family style.

RADISH, ORANGE, AND AVOCADO SALAD

THE HUGELY DIFFERENT TEXTURES IN THIS SALAD—CREAMY
AVOCADO, CRUNCHY RADISH, AND JUICY ORANGE—WORK
AMAZINGLY WELL TOGETHER.

YIELD: 4 SERVINGS

2 tablespoons freshly squeezed
   lemon juice
2 tablespoons extra-virgin olive oil
1 large ripe Haas avocado, pitted,
   peeled, and cut into 1-inch cubes
2 large seedless oranges
1 bunch (6 to 8) red radishes,
   thinly sliced
Coarse sea salt or kosher salt and
   freshly milled black pepper

1. In a salad bowl, whisk together the lemon juice and olive oil. Add the avocado and toss gently.

2. Cut the rind off the oranges until no pith remains. Cut the oranges from blossom to stem end into quarters then cut crosswise into ½-inch slices. Add the orange slices and radishes to the bowl. Season with salt and pepper and toss. Serve immediately.

BLACK BEAN TOSTADAS WITH CHERRY TOMATO SALSA

SEITAN IS A WONDERFUL MEAT SUBSTITUTE IN TERMS OF TEXTURE, AND IT'S AVAILABLE READY-MADE. YOU CAN USE FRESH STORE BOUGHT TOSTADAS, BUT THEY'RE BETTER IF YOU MAKE THEM YOURSELF. ALL YOU DO IS BRUSH FRESH TORTILLAS WITH OIL AND BAKE THEM IN A 350°F OVEN FOR 10 TO 12 MINUTES UNTIL CRISP.

YIELD: 4 SERVINGS

For the cherry tomato salsa

1 pint cherry tomatoes, stemmed and quartered

1 small red onion, finely chopped

½ cup chopped fresh cilantro

Juice of 2 limes

1 jalapeño pepper (with seeds), finely chopped

Coarse sea salt or kosher salt and freshly
    milled black pepper

For the tostadas

3 tablespoons extra-virgin olive oil

1 small onion, chopped

2 garlic cloves, finely chopped

1 tablespoon cumin seeds, freshly ground

½ teaspoon dried oregano

1 (15-ounce) can black beans

1 (8 ounce) package seitan, finely
    chopped (see Note on page 163)

1 chipotle pepper in adobo sauce, chopped

1 tablespoon soy sauce

Coarse sea salt or kosher salt and
    freshly milled black pepper

8 tostada shells

Shredded romaine lettuce for serving

Sour cream for serving

1. To prepare the salsa, in a serving bowl, toss together the tomatoes, onion, cilantro, lime juice, and jalapeño. Season with salt and refrigerate until serving time.

2. To prepare the tostadas, in a large sauté pan over high heat, warm the oil. Add the onion, garlic, cumin, and oregano and sauté until the onion is lightly browned, about 3 minutes.

3. Stir in the black beans and their liquid, the seitan, chipotle pepper and its sauce, and soy sauce and bring to a boil. Cook until the mixture thickens, about 5 minutes, then season with salt and pepper.

4. To serve: place the beans, salsa, lettuce, and sour cream in separate bowls and allow each diner to assemble their tostadas at the table.

GILDING THE LILY

If you are feeling ambitious, try making your own seitan. It does not require any special skills or equipment, and homemade seitan freezes beautifully for up to 4 months without any loss in taste or texture. For a complete guide to making seitan, refer to my first book, *The Modern Vegetarian Kitchen.*

MENU 3

•

ROMAINE SALAD WITH SUN-DRIED TOMATOES AND LEMON-PARMESAN DRESSING

•

WEHANI AND WILD RICE STEW WITH CREMINI MUSHROOMS, WINTER SQUASH, AND KALE

MARKET LIST

FRESH PRODUCE
3 hearts of romaine
    lettuce
1 small bunch kale
Celery
1 ½ to 2 pounds
    winter squash such as
    butternut, buttercup, or
    Hokkaido
½ pound cremini
    mushrooms
1 medium carrot
1 large onion
Ginger
Garlic
Sage
1 lemon

DAIRY
Unsalted butter
4 ounces Parmesan
    cheese

PANTRY
Extra-virgin olive oil
Soy sauce
Dijon-style mustard
4 ounces shelled pumpkin
    seeds (optional)
4 ounces Wehani rice or
    long-grain brown rice
4 ounces wild rice
Sun-dried tomatoes
Coarse sea salt or
    kosher salt
Black peppercorns
1 loaf crusty bread

EQUIPMENT
Large skillet with lid
Pressure cooker
Box grater
Wire whisk
Citrus juicer

MENU 3 GAME PLAN
1. Prepare the stew through
    step 1.
2. Prepare the salad
    dressing.
3. Prepare the salad greens
    and refrigerate them.
4. Finish the stew.
5. Toast the pumpkin seeds
    if using.
6. Finish the salad.
7. Serve the salad and stew
    with crusty bread.

ROMAINE SALAD WITH SUN-DRIED TOMATOES AND LEMON-PARMESAN DRESSING

YOU CAN BUY SUN-DRIED TOMATOES IN BULK AS YOU WOULD DRIED FRUIT, OR PACKED IN OIL IN JARS. IF YOU'RE BUYING THE BULK KIND IT'S IMPORTANT TO PURCHASE ONES THAT ARE FRESH AND SUPPLE, WITH A TEXTURE SIMILAR TO DRIED APRICOTS. IF THEY'RE REALLY DESICCATED, THEY'LL NEED TO BE RECONSTITUTED IN WATER, WHICH CAN MAKE THEM MUSHY. SO IF YOU CAN'T FIND GOOD-QUALITY BULK SUN-DRIED TOMATOES, USE OIL-PACKED INSTEAD.

YIELD: 4 SERVINGS

1 garlic clove, halved

3 hearts of romaine lettuce, torn into bite-sized pieces

5 sun-dried tomatoes, drained if oil-packed, cut into strips

2 tablespoons freshly squeezed lemon juice

2 tablespoons grated Parmesan cheese, plus additional for garnish

1 tablespoon Dijon-style mustard

Coarse sea salt or kosher salt and freshly milled black pepper

⅓ cup extra-virgin olive oil

1. Rub the inside of a salad bowl vigorously with the garlic halves. Add the romaine and sun-dried tomatoes.

2. In a small bowl, whisk together lemon juice, Parmesan, and mustard. Season generously with salt and pepper, then slowly whisk in the oil.

3. Toss the salad with the dressing and sprinkle with additional grated cheese.

WEHANI AND WILD RICE STEW WITH CREMINI MUSHROOMS, WINTER SQUASH, AND KALE

WEHANI RICE HAS AN AROMA LIKE POPCORN AND A LOVELY RED COLOR. WHEN COMBINED WITH NUTTY WILD RICE, THE TWO MIX WELL TO CREATE A VERY SPECIAL, DEEPLY EARTHY FLAVOR. HOWEVER, YOU CAN ALSO EXPERIMENT WITH ANY MIXTURE OF WHOLE GRAIN RICES, AND CAN LIKEWISE SUBSTITUTE ANY OTHER TYPE OF MUSHROOM FOR THE CREMINI.

YIELD: **4** TO **6** SERVINGS

⅓ cup Wehani rice

⅓ cup wild rice

1 (1-inch) piece fresh ginger, unpeeled,
    sliced into thick rounds

2 garlic cloves, peeled

1 teaspoon coarse sea salt or kosher salt

2 tablespoons unsalted butter or
    extra-virgin olive oil

1 large onion, diced

½ pound cremini mushrooms,
    cleaned and thickly sliced

1 stalk celery, diced

1 medium carrot, peeled and thinly sliced

2 tablespoons minced fresh sage

1 small or ½ large winter squash, peeled, seeded,
    and cut into 1-inch chunks (about 4 cups)

1 small bunch kale, tough stems discarded, leaves
    sliced into thin strips (4 cups)

1 to 2 tablespoons soy sauce

Freshly milled black pepper

Extra-virgin olive oil for serving

½ cup toasted pumpkin seeds
    (optional, see page 7)

1. In a pressure cooker, combine 4 cups of water, the Wehani and wild rice, ginger, garlic, and salt. Secure the lid and bring to full pressure over high heat. Reduce the heat to medium-low and cook for 30 minutes.

2. While the rice cooks, in a large skillet over high heat, melt the butter or warm the oil. Add the onion, mushrooms, celery, carrot, and sage and sauté until well browned, about 10 minutes. Add 1 cup of water and scrape up the brown bits from the bottom of the pan with a wooden spoon. Add the squash, cover the pan, and simmer until tender, 8 to 10 minutes.

3. Transfer the pressure cooker to the sink and run cold water over it to bring down the pressure. Return the cooker to medium heat. Add the vegetables from the skillet and the kale and simmer, uncovered, until the kale is tender, about 3 minutes.

4. Season the stew with soy sauce and pepper. Serve in wide soup bowls, drizzled with olive oil and sprinkled with toasted pumpkin seeds, if desired.

MENU 4

RED LENTIL AND
SWEET POTATO CURRY
WITH WARM PITA BREAD

SPICY RED CABBAGE
WITH CUMIN SEEDS
AND TOMATOES

MARKET LIST

FRESH PRODUCE
1 small head red cabbage
1 medium sweet potato
2 medium shallots
1 medium onion
Ginger
Garlic
Cilantro
1 lemon

DAIRY
Unsalted butter

PANTRY
Neutral vegetable oil,
    such as canola,
    grapeseed, or sunflower
Extra-virgin olive oil
Cumin seeds
Crushed red pepper
    flakes
Bay leaves
Curry powder
1 pound red lentils
1 (14-ounce) can whole or
    diced tomatoes, packed
    in juice
4 ounces raisins
Coarse sea salt or
    kosher salt
1 package pita bread
    (whole wheat or white)

EQUIPMENT
Large sauté pan with lid
Large saucepan with lid
Small saucepan or kettle
Citrus juicer

MENU 4 GAME PLAN
1. Preheat the oven to
   300°F.
2. Prepare the curry.
3. Cook the cabbage.
4. Warm the pita bread.
5. Serve family style.

RED LENTIL AND SWEET POTATO CURRY WITH WARM PITA BREAD

RED LENTILS ARE SMALL PEELED LENTILS THAT ARE COMMONLY USED FOR INDIAN DAL BECAUSE THEY COOK QUICKLY AND TURN INTO A SMOOTH, LUSCIOUS SAUCE. HERE I COMBINE THEM WITH SWEET POTATOES IN A LIGHTLY SPICED CURRY. YOU CAN SERVE IT OVER RICE OR WITH LAVASH INSTEAD OF PITA.

YIELD: **4** SERVINGS

2 tablespoons neutral oil, such as
   canola, grapeseed or sunflower
1 medium onion, chopped
Coarse sea salt or kosher salt
1 medium sweet potato, peeled and cut
   into 1-inch chunks (about 4 cups)
1 (1-inch) piece fresh ginger,
   peeled and chopped
1 large or 2 small garlic cloves, chopped
1 tablespoon curry powder
1 bay leaf
1 ½ cups red lentils
Pita bread

1. Preheat the oven to 300°F. In a saucepan or kettle, bring 3 ½ cups of water to a boil.

2. In a large saucepan over high heat, warm the oil. Add the onion and a pinch of salt and sauté, stirring occasionally, until the onion softens, about 3 to 4 minutes.

3. Add the sweet potato, ginger, garlic, curry powder, and bay leaf and sauté until fragrant, about 1 minute. Pour in the boiling water and stir in the lentils. Reduce the heat to medium-low, cover, and simmer until the lentils break down and the sweet potatoes are tender, 18 to 20 minutes. Season with salt.

4. While the potatoes and lentils are cooking, wrap a stack of pita breads in a slightly damp cotton towel, and place in oven for 10 to 15 minutes.

5. Serve the curry with the warm pita bread and spicy cabbage.

SPICY RED CABBAGE WITH CUMIN SEEDS AND TOMATOES

THIS AROMATIC DISH HAS A SLIGHT SWEETNESS FROM THE RAISINS. IT'S MY TAKE ON A TRADITIONAL INDIAN CABBAGE RECIPE.

YIELD: **4** SERVINGS

2 tablespoons unsalted butter

2 teaspoons cumin seeds

2 medium shallots, thinly sliced

1 teaspoon crushed red pepper flakes, or to taste

½ small head red cabbage, cored and sliced into thin strips (about 3 cups)

1 (14-ounce) can whole or diced tomatoes with their juice

⅓ cup raisins

½ teaspoon coarse sea salt or kosher salt

Juice of 1 lemon

½ cup chopped fresh cilantro

1. In a large sauté pan over medium heat, melt the butter. Add the cumin seeds and sauté for 1 minute. Add the shallots and red pepper flakes and sauté for 2 minutes, stirring frequently.

2. Add the cabbage, tomatoes and their liquid, and raisins. If using whole tomatoes, crush them against the side of the pan with the back of a wooden spoon. Raise the heat and bring the mixture to a boil. Add the ½ teaspoon of salt, reduce the heat to low, and simmer, covered, until the cabbage is tender, 8 to 10 minutes. Stir in the lemon juice and cilantro. Season with additional salt if desired, and serve.

SOMETHING EXTRA

Serve small dishes of lightly salted yogurt as a refreshing accompaniment to this spicy meal.

MENU 5

•

BARLEY RISOTTO WITH GOLDEN BEETS, SWISS CHARD, AND GOAT CHEESE

•

FENNEL-CABBAGE SLAW WITH RAISINS AND APPLE

MARKET LIST

FRESH PRODUCE
1 bunch Swiss chard
1 large bulb fennel
1 small green cabbage
3 medium golden beets
1 medium onion
Ginger
Rosemary
2 lemons
1 red apple

DAIRY
4 ounces fresh goat cheese
4 ounces Parmesan cheese

PANTRY
Extra-virgin olive oil
Fennel seeds
8 ounces pearl barley
2 ounces raisins
Coarse sea salt or kosher salt
Black peppercorns

EQUIPMENT
Small saucepan or kettle
Pressure cooker
Box grater
Wire whisk
Citrus juicer

MENU 5 GAME PLAN
1. Prepare the slaw and chill.
2. Prepare the risotto.
3. Serve the risotto with cheese on the side, accompanied by the slaw.

BARLEY RISOTTO WITH GOLDEN BEETS, SWISS CHARD, AND GOAT CHEESE

THE CHARM OF THIS RISOTTO IS IN THE SUBTLE WARM COLOR OF GOLDEN BEETS. IF YOU CANNOT FIND GOLDEN BEETS, YOU CAN USE RED ONES INSTEAD. THEY WILL STILL WORK BEAUTIFULLY, BUT YOU'LL WIND UP WITH SOMETHING MORE DRAMATIC AND CRIMSON IN COLOR. TART GOAT CHEESE PLAYS OFF THE SWEET BEETS AND MAKES AN INSTANT CREAMY SAUCE AS YOU STIR IT IN.

YIELD: 4 SERVINGS

2 tablespoons extra-virgin olive oil
1 cup diced onion
1 teaspoon coarse sea salt or kosher salt,
    plus additional to taste
1 cup pearl barley
1 tablespoon peeled and minced fresh ginger
2 teaspoons minced fresh rosemary
3 medium golden beets, peeled and cut into ½-inch dice
4 cups thinly sliced Swiss chard leaves
4 ounces fresh goat cheese, cut into 1-inch pieces
Freshly milled black pepper
Grated Parmesan cheese for serving

1. In a saucepan or kettle, bring 3 cups of water to a boil.

2. In a pressure cooker over high heat, warm the oil. Add the onion and 1 teaspoon of salt and sauté for 2 minutes. Add the barley, ginger, and rosemary and sauté, stirring, for 1 minute. Add the beets and the boiling water. Lock the lid in place and bring to full pressure. Lower the heat to medium and let cook for 9 minutes.

3. Transfer the pot to the sink and run cold water over it to bring down the pressure.

4. Return the pot to the stove top and stir in the chard. Cook, uncovered, over medium heat, until the chard has softened, about 1 minute. Stir in the goat cheese and cook until it melts into the risotto, about 2 minutes longer. Season with salt and pepper and serve immediately with Parmesan cheese.

FENNEL-CABBAGE SLAW WITH RAISINS AND APPLE

FOR ME, CABBAGE IS THE MOST VERSATILE OF
VEGETABLES AND THE ONE I INSIST FOLLOWS ME INTO THE
NEXT WORLD. THIS HUMBLE (AND OFTEN MALIGNED)
CRUCIFER REVEALS ITS MANY CHARMS WHETHER PICKLED,
STEAMED, BRAISED, SAUTÉED, STUFFED, OR RAW, AS IN
THIS REFRESHING AUTUMN SALAD.

YIELD: **4** SERVINGS

3 tablespoons extra-virgin olive oil

3 tablespoons freshly squeezed lemon juice

1 teaspoon fennel seeds, toasted
    and ground (see page 8)

Coarse sea salt or kosher salt and freshly
    milled black pepper

1 large bulb fennel, trimmed and sliced
    paper thin, fronds chopped

½ small head green cabbage, thinly sliced
    (about 3 cups)

1 red apple, unpeeled, cored and cut
    into matchsticks

3 tablespoons raisins

1. In a salad bowl, whisk together the oil, lemon juice, and ground fennel seeds. Season with salt and pepper.

2. Add the fennel, cabbage, apple, and raisins and toss to combine. Refrigerate for 15 minutes. Season with additional salt and pepper and serve.

MENU 6

PASTA WITH
SPICY CAULIFLOWER,
CHICKPEAS, AND
CHERRY TOMATOES

PAN-GRILLED
RADICCHIO SALAD
WITH HONEY-
BALSAMIC GLAZE

MARKET LIST

FRESH PRODUCE

1 large or 2 medium
   heads frisée or 1 head
   curly endive
1 large head radicchio
2 pints cherry tomatoes
2 small delicata squash
   (about 1 pound total)
1 small cauliflower
2 medium carrots
2 medium red onions
1 small shallot
Garlic
Thyme
Flat-leaf parsley
1 lemon

DAIRY

4 ounces Parmesan cheese

PANTRY

Extra-virgin olive oil
Balsamic vinegar
Saffron threads
Cumin seeds
Crushed red pepper flakes
Honey
8 ounces penne or
   rigatoni pasta
1 (15-ounce) can
   chickpeas
Coarse sea salt or
   kosher salt
Black peppercorns
Dry white wine, such as
   Pinot Grigio or
   Sauvignon Blanc

EQUIPMENT

Large pot
Large nonstick skillet
Salad spinner
Colander
Rimmed baking sheet or
   large roasting pan
Box grater
Slotted spoon
Wire whisk
Citrus juicer

MENU 6 GAME PLAN

1. Place a baking pan on the
   middle shelf of the oven
   and preheat to 500°F.
   Bring a pot of water to a
   boil for the pasta.
2. Prepare the pasta
   through step 3.
3. Wash and cut the salad
   greens.
4. Boil the pasta.
5. Finish the salad.
6. Finish the pasta.
7. Serve the pasta
   accompanied by the
   salad.

PASTA WITH SPICY CAULIFLOWER, CHICKPEAS, AND CHERRY TOMATOES

THIS IS A VERY UNUSUAL RECIPE BECAUSE YOU MAKE THE
SAUCE ON A BAKING SHEET. BUT THAT LARGE SURFACE AREA
IS WHAT MAKES IT COOK SO FAST, AND THE HIGH HEAT OF
THE OVEN CARAMELIZES AND INTENSIFIES THE FLAVORS.

YIELD: **4** SERVINGS

Large pinch of saffron threads
3 tablespoons coarse sea salt or
    kosher salt, plus additional to taste
1 small cauliflower (or ½ a large
    one), separated into florets
2 medium red onions, peeled and
    cut into 1-inch-thick wedges
2 medium carrots, peeled and
    sliced on the bias into 1-inch pieces
2 small delicata squash, halved lengthwise,
    seeded, and cut into thin half moons
1 (15-ounce) can chickpeas, drained
2 pints cherry tomatoes, halved
¾ cup dry white wine
½ cup extra-virgin olive oil
4 garlic cloves, thinly sliced
1 tablespoon cumin seeds, toasted
    and ground (see page 8) or
    1 tablespoon ground cumin
½ teaspoon crushed red pepper flakes
3 sprigs fresh thyme
½ pound penne or rigatoni pasta
Freshly milled black pepper
½ cup freshly grated Parmesan cheese
¼ cup chopped fresh flat-leaf parsley

1. Set a rimmed baking sheet or large roasting pan on the middle shelf of the oven and preheat to 500°F (the pan should be large enough to hold the vegetables in a single layer).

2. Bring a large pot of water to a boil. In a small dish, combine 1 tablespoon of the boiling water with the saffron and set aside. Add the 3 tablespoons of salt to the pot. Add the cauliflower, onions, carrots, and squash to the pot and cover it until it returns to a boil. Uncover and cook the vegetables for 2 minutes. Using a slotted spoon, transfer the vegetables to a colander to drain, saving the cooking water.

3. In a large bowl, toss the blanched vegetables with the chickpeas, cherry tomatoes, wine, oil, garlic, cumin, red pepper flakes, thyme, and saffron with its soaking liquid. Transfer the mixture to the hot pan in the oven and roast for 15 minutes, stirring midway through the cooking time, until the vegetables are tender and lightly caramelized. Discard the thyme sprigs.

4. While the vegetables are roasting, return the pot of water to a boil. Add the pasta and cook until al dente. Drain well and transfer to a wide serving bowl. Toss the pasta with the vegetables and season with salt and pepper. Garnish with cheese and parsley and serve immediately.

PAN-GRILLED RADICCHIO SALAD WITH HONEY-BALSAMIC GLAZE

THIS UNIQUE, WARM AUTUMNAL SALAD FALLS
SOMEWHERE BETWEEN A COOKED VEGETABLE AND
A TRADITIONAL SALAD.

YIELD: **4** SERVINGS

3 tablespoons balsamic vinegar
1 small shallot, finely chopped
1 large head radicchio
5 tablespoons plus 1 teaspoon extra-
    virgin olive oil
1 tablespoon honey
Coarse sea salt or kosher salt and
    freshly milled black pepper
4 cups bite-sized pieces frisée or curly endive
1 tablespoon freshly squeezed lemon juice

1. In a small bowl, combined the vinegar and shallot and set aside.

2. Slice the radicchio through the stem end into 4 wedges.

3. In a large nonstick skillet over high heat, warm 1 teaspoon of the oil. Place the radicchio wedges on one of their flat sides in the pan and cook, undisturbed, until golden brown, about 2 minutes. Turn the radicchio wedges and brown on the other side.

4. Meanwhile, whisk 4 tablespoons of the oil and the honey into the vinegar and shallot mixture. Season with salt and pepper.

5. Pour the vinaigrette over the radicchio and cook for 1 minute.

6. In a salad bowl, toss the frisée with the lemon juice and the remaining tablespoon of olive oil.

7. Mound the frisée in the center of each plate. Place a wedge of radicchio next to the frisée and drizzle with pan juices.

MENU 7

•

PUMPKIN, PEAR, AND FENNEL SOUP

•

QUINOA WITH BRUSSELS SPROUTS, TEMPEH, AND TOASTED ALMONDS

MARKET LIST

FRESH PRODUCE

1 pound winter squash

1 red bell pepper

1 pound Brussels sprouts

2 medium leeks

4 medium onions

Ginger

1 lemon

1 pound ripe Bartlett or
   Anjou pears (2 large or 3
   small pears)

DAIRY AND PERISHABLES

Unsalted butter

Crème fraîche or yogurt

1 (8-ounce) package soy
   tempeh

Apple cider (optional)

PANTRY

Extra-virgin olive oil

Soy sauce

Mirin

Fennel seeds

Caraway seeds (optional)

Ground cinnamon

12 ounces quinoa

Coarse sea salt or
   kosher salt

Black peppercorns

4 ounces almonds

EQUIPMENT

Large sauté pan with lid

Medium saucepan with lid

Pressure cooker

Blender

MENU 7 GAME PLAN

1. Preheat the oven to
   350°F.
2. Cook the quinoa for the
   braise.
3. Prepare the soup through
   step 3.
4. Toast the almonds for the
   braise.
5. Braise the tempeh and
   vegetables.
6. Finish the soup.
7. Slice a lemon for
   garnishing the braise.
8. Serve the soup.
9. Serve the braise over the
   quinoa, garnished with
   almonds and a lemon
   slice.

PUMPKIN, PEAR, AND FENNEL SOUP

ONE OF THE UNIQUE CHARACTERISTICS OF FENNEL SEED IS
THAT IT BRINGS OUT THE NATURAL SWEETNESS IN OTHER
INGREDIENTS. HERE IT WORKS ITS MAGIC ON THE PUMPKIN
AND PEAR IN THIS CREAMY SOUP.

YIELD: 4 SERVINGS

2 tablespoons unsalted butter
2 medium leeks, white and tender
    green parts only, cleaned (see page 61)
    and thinly sliced
½ teaspoon coarse sea salt or
    kosher salt, plus additional to taste
4 cups winter squash, peeled and roughly
    chopped (1-inch chunks)
1 pound ripe Bartlett or Anjou pears
    (2 large or 3 small pears), cored and sliced
1 tablespoon peeled and minced fresh ginger
2 teaspoons fennel seed, toasted and ground
    (see page 8)
Apple cider (optional)
Freshly milled black pepper
Crème fraîche or yogurt for garnish
Ground cinnamon for garnish

1. In a pressure cooker over medium heat, melt the butter. Add the leeks and the ½ teaspoon of salt. Sauté until softened, about 2 minutes.

2. Add the squash, pears, ginger, ground fennel, and 3 cups of water. Secure the lid, raise the heat, and bring to full pressure. Reduce the heat to low and simmer for 8 minutes.

3. Transfer the pot to the sink and run cold water over it to bring down the pressure.

4. Using an immersion blender, or in batches in a blender, puree the soup until creamy. Thin the soup with apple cider or water if it is too thick, and season with salt and pepper to taste. Serve with a dollop of crème fraîche or yogurt and a sprinkle of ground cinnamon.

QUINOA WITH BRUSSELS SPROUTS, TEMPEH, AND TOASTED ALMONDS

QUINOA IS YET ANOTHER ANCIENT FAST-COOKING WHOLE GRAIN THAT IS ACTUALLY A COMPLETE PROTEIN. ITS DISTINCTIVE NUTTY FLAVOR IS COMPLEMENTED BY THE TEMPEH AND ALMONDS AND ROUNDED OUT BY THE BRUSSELS SPROUTS.

YIELD: **4** SERVINGS

For the quinoa

1 tablespoon unsalted butter

½ teaspoon coarse sea salt or kosher salt

1 ½ cups quinoa

For the Brussels sprouts and tempeh

⅓ cup extra-virgin olive oil

2 cups thinly sliced onions

½ teaspoon caraway seeds (optional)

1 (8 ounce) package soy tempeh, sliced
 into bite-sized pieces

1 red bell pepper, seeded and thinly sliced

1 pound Brussels sprouts, trimmed and
 cut lengthwise into thirds

¼ cup soy sauce

2 tablespoons mirin (see page 135)

Coarse sea salt or kosher salt and
 freshly milled black pepper

½ cup chopped toasted almonds
 (see page 7)

Lemon wedges for serving

1. To prepare the quinoa, in a medium saucepan over high heat, combine the butter and salt with 2 ½ cups of water and bring to a boil. Reduce the heat to low and stir in the quinoa. Cover the pot and simmer for 18 minutes.

2. Turn off the heat and set aside, covered, for 3 minutes. Fluff with a fork before serving.

3. To prepare the Bussels sprouts, in a large sauté pan over medium heat, warm the oil. Add the onion and caraway seeds, if using, and sauté for 2 minutes.

4. Raise the heat and add the tempeh and peppers. Cook, stirring occasionally, until the tempeh begins to caramelize, about 2 minutes.

5. Add the Brussels sprouts, 1 cup of water, the soy sauce, and mirin and bring to a boil. Reduce the heat and simmer, covered, for 10 minutes. Season with salt and pepper to taste.

6. Serve the Brussels sprouts over the quinoa, sprinkled with toasted almonds and accompanied by lemon wedges.

MENU 8

•

GIANT AREPAS WITH AGED GOUDA

•

BRAISED PINTO BEANS WITH DELICATA SQUASH, RED WINE, AND TOMATOES

MARKET LIST

FRESH PRODUCE

1 pound delicata squash
1 red bell pepper
1 medium jalapeño pepper
1 medium green cabbage
2 carrots
1 bunch red radishes
2 large onions
Garlic
Sage
2 bunches cilantro
3 limes
1 bunch scallions

DAIRY

Unsalted butter
16 ounces sour cream
4 ounces aged Gouda or Monterey Jack cheese

PANTRY

Extra-virgin olive oil
Neutral oil, such as grapeseed, canola, or sunflower
Sugar, preferably organic washed cane sugar (see page 8)
1 ½ pounds masa harina
1 (15-ounce) can pinto beans
1 (14-ounce) can whole or diced tomatoes packed in juice
1 chipotle chili in adobo sauce
Coarse sea salt or kosher salt
Black peppercorns
Dry red wine, such as San Giovese, Merlot, or Zinfandel

EQUIPMENT

Large pot
Large sauté pan with lid
1 large or 2 small skillets
Rimmed baking sheet
Box grater
Whisk

MENU 8 GAME PLAN

1. Preheat the oven to 250°F.
2. Prepare the braise.
3. Prepare the picadillo.
4. Prepare the arepas.
5. Place the arepas on plates and smother with the braise. Top with sour cream and sprigs of cilantro.

GIANT AREPAS WITH AGED GOUDA

HERE IS A LARGER AND MORE FLAVORFUL VARIATION ON TRADITIONAL AREPAS (SEE PAGE 107). I USE AGED GOUDA, BUT YOU CAN SUBSTITUTE MONTEREY JACK OR A SHARP CHEDDAR IF YOU PREFER.

YIELD: **4** SERVINGS

3 cups masa harina (see page 107)
4 ounces aged Gouda or Monterey Jack cheese,
  coarsely grated
2 teaspoons coarse sea salt or kosher salt
Neutral oil, such as grapeseed, canola or
  sunflower, for frying
Sour cream for garnish
Cilantro sprigs for garnish

1. Preheat the oven to 250°F.

2. Place a rimmed baking sheet in the oven. In a large bowl, combine the masa, cheese, and salt. Add 3 cups of water and mix well. Cover the bowl with plastic wrap or a plate and set aside for 5 minutes.

3. Form the dough into 4 balls.

4. In a large skillet over high heat, warm 1 tablespoon of oil (or divide the oil between 2 small skillets).

5. Take one ball and slap it between your palms to flatten it into a 6-inch round. Place the dough in the skillet and reduce the heat to medium. Cook until golden and crispy, about 3 minutes per side. Transfer the cooked arepa to the pan in the oven to keep warm. Repeat with remaining pieces of dough, adding more oil if necessary.

6. To serve, ladle the pinto beans and squash over the arepas and top with sour cream and sprigs of cilantro.

BRAISED PINTO BEANS WITH DELICATA SQUASH, RED WINE, AND TOMATOES

DELICATA SQUASH IS WONDERFULLY CONVENIENT SINCE ITS SKIN IS BEAUTIFUL TO THE EYE AND TENDER TO THE TOOTH. THE SQUASH ALSO TEND TO BE SMALL—HALF A POUND TO A POUND ON AVERAGE. THEY ARE EASY TO HANDLE, AND SLICED IN HALF LENGTHWISE, THEY SEED EASILY.

YIELD: **4** SERVINGS

1 tablespoon unsalted butter
1 tablespoon extra-virgin olive oil
2 cups thinly sliced onion
1 teaspoon coarse sea salt or kosher
   salt, plus additional to taste
1 pound delicata squash, halved, seeded,
   and cut into ½-inch-thick slices
3 garlic cloves, thinly sliced
1 (15-ounce) can pinto beans
1 (14-ounce) can whole or diced
   tomatoes with their juice
⅓ cup dry red wine, such as San Giovese,
   Merlot, or Zinfandel
1 chipotle chile in adobo sauce, chopped
1 tablespoon chopped fresh sage
Freshly milled black pepper

1. In a large sauté pan over high heat, melt the butter with the oil. Add the onion and 1 teaspoon of salt and sauté until lightly browned, about 5 minutes. Reduce the heat, add the squash and garlic, and sauté for 1 minute.

2. Stir in the pinto beans and their liquid, tomatoes and their juice, wine, chipotle, and sage. Raise the heat and bring to a boil. If using whole tomatoes, crush them against the side of the pan with the back of a wooden spoon. Reduce the heat and simmer, covered, until the squash is tender, but not falling apart, about 15 minutes.

3. Uncover the pan and cook for 1 to 2 minutes to thicken the sauce. Season with salt and pepper and serve over arepas.

PICADILLO

THIS SAVORY AND HEARTY MENU BENEFITS FROM THE ZESTY
AND REFRESHING CRUNCH OF PICADILLO, A SLIGHTLY SPICY
SPANISH DISH, USUALLY MADE WITH VARIOUS MARINATED MEATS
AND VEGETABLES. THIS VEGETARIAN VERSION IS AN EXCELLENT
ACCOMPANIMENT TO THE AREPAS AND THE BEANS AND SQUASH.

YIELD: **4** SERVINGS

2 tablespoons coarse sea salt or kosher salt,
   plus additional to taste
½ medium green cabbage, roughly chopped
   (about 6 cups)
¼ cup freshly squeezed lime juice
2 tablespoons extra-virgin olive oil
2 garlic cloves, minced
1 medium jalapeño pepper, with seeds, minced
½ teaspoon sugar, preferably organic
   washed cane sugar (see page 8)
Freshly milled black pepper
1 cup thinly sliced peeled carrot
1 red bell pepper, seeded and thinly sliced
1 bunch red radishes, thinly sliced
1 cup roughly chopped cilantro stems and leaves
2 scallions, thinly sliced

1. Fill a large bowl with ice water.

2. Bring a pot of water to a boil and add 2 tablespoons of
salt. When the water returns to a boil, add the cabbage
and boil for 1 minute. Drain the cabbage and transfer it to
the ice water to stop the cooking. Drain thoroughly and
blot with a towel.

3. In a large bowl, whisk together the lime juice, oil, garlic,
jalapeño, and sugar. Season with salt and pepper. Add the
blanched cabbage, carrot, pepper, radishes, cilantro, and
scallions and toss to combine.

MENU 9

•

ROASTED WINTER SQUASH WITH CURRY BUTTER AND APPLE CIDER

•

STUFFED GREENS WITH RED BEAN AND VEGETABLES RAGOUT

MARKET LIST

FRESH PRODUCE

1 large head romaine lettuce
Celery
2 pounds winter squash
1 small jalapeño pepper
Scallions
1 medium red onion
Garlic

DAIRY AND PERISHABLES

Unsalted butter
2 large eggs
4 ounces Parmesan cheese
6 ounces whole-milk ricotta cheese
8 ounces apple cider

PANTRY

Extra-virgin olive oil
Cumin seeds or ground cumin
Hot curry powder
Unrefined brown sugar, such as Sucanat
1 (15-ounce) can red kidney beans
1 (14-ounce) can whole peeled tomatoes packed in juice
Coarse sea salt or kosher salt
Black peppercorns
2 slices day-old country sourdough bread
Dry white wine, such as Sauvignon Blanc or Pinot Grigio

EQUIPMENT

Large sauté pan with lid
Large saucepan
Ovenproof casserole
Food processor
Salad spinner

MENU 9 GAME PLAN

1. Preheat the oven to 400°F.
2. Boil water for blanching the romaine.
3. Roast the squash.
4. Prepare the stuffed romaine and ragout.
5. Serve the romaine parcels in wide soup plates topped with ragout and sprinkled with chopped parsley. Serve the squash on the side.

ROASTED WINTER SQUASH WITH CURRY BUTTER AND APPLE CIDER

MY FAVORITE WINTER SQUASH ARE DELICATA, RED KURI, BUTTERCUP, AND HOKKAIDO. ALL HAVE SMOOTH, DENSE FLESH AND TENDER SKINS, WHICH DO NOT REQUIRE PEELING.

YIELD: **4** SERVINGS

3 tablespoons unsalted butter

2 tablespoons unrefined brown sugar, such as Sucanat (see page 8)

1 tablespoon hot curry powder

¼ teaspoon coarse sea or kosher salt

2 pounds winter squash, peeled if necessary, seeded, and cut into 2-inch chunks

1 cup apple cider

1. Preheat the oven to 450°F. Select an ovenproof casserole or skillet large enough to hold the squash in a single layer.

2. Melt the butter in the casserole over medium heat. Add the brown sugar, curry powder, and salt, and cook, stirring, until the butter melts. Add the squash and toss to coat.

3. Gradually pour the cider down the side of the pan without pouring it directly over the squash. Increase the heat to high and bring to a boil.

4. Transfer the casserole to the oven and roast for 30 minutes, basting midway through the cooking time. The squash is done when the tip of a knife does not meet with any resistance when inserted into the squash.

STUFFED GREENS WITH RED BEAN AND VEGETABLES RAGOUT

THIS RECIPE MAY SEEM A LITTLE MORE INVOLVED THAN MOST IN THIS BOOK, BUT IT'S REALLY QUITE EASY. THE ROMAINE LETTUCE LEAVES COOK RAPIDLY, MAINTAIN THEIR SHAPE, AND UNLIKE CABBAGE, ARE VERY EASY TO FILL AND ROLL. IT'S A HEARTY AUTUMN DISH THAT WILL COOK UP WHILE YOU PREPARE THE SALAD.

YIELD: **4** SERVINGS

1 tablespoon coarse sea salt or kosher salt
8 large leaves romaine lettuce

For the stuffing
2 slices day-old country sourdough bread
¾ cup whole-milk ricotta cheese
1 large egg
1 large egg yolk
½ cup freshly grated Parmesan cheese

For the beans
¼ cup extra-virgin olive oil
1 medium red onion, chopped
1 stalk celery with leaves, thinly sliced
1 teaspoon coarse sea salt or kosher salt
½ small jalapeño pepper, with seeds, finely chopped,
   or ¼ teaspoon crushed red pepper flakes
1 garlic clove, thinly sliced
½ teaspoon cumin seeds, toasted and ground
   (see page 8) or ¾ teaspoon ground cumin
1 (14-ounce) can whole peeled tomatoes
   with their juice
1 (15-ounce) can kidney beans, drained
⅓ cup dry white wine, such as Sauvignon Blanc
   or Pinot Grigio
1 scallion, thinly sliced, for garnish

1. In a large saucepan, bring 2 quarts of water to a boil, then add the salt.

2. Wash the romaine leaves, add them to the boiling water, and blanch for 15 seconds. Drain thoroughly and blot with a towel.

3. To prepare the stuffing, in the bowl of a food processor fitted with a metal blade, process the bread slices into crumbs and transfer to a large measuring cup. Return 1 firmly packed cup of bread crumbs to the food processor (discard any extra bread crumbs or reserve for another use). Add the ricotta cheese, egg, egg yolk, and Parmesan and pulse a few times to combine. Transfer the mixture to a bowl and set aside.

4. To prepare the beans, in a large sauté pan over medium heat, warm the oil. Add the onion, celery, and salt and sauté for 3 minutes. Add the jalapeño, garlic, and cumin and sauté for 2 more minutes. Add the tomatoes and their juice, crushing them with the back of a spoon against the side of the pan. Stir in the beans and wine. Raise the heat and bring the mixture to a boil. Cover the pan, turn off the heat, and let cool slightly.

5. With moist hands, form the breadcrumb stuffing into 8 equal mounds. Lay a blanched romaine leaf on a clean surface and cut off the base if it is large. Place a mound of stuffing in the bottom third of the leaf and fold up the bottom to cover it. Fold the sides of the leaf into the center then roll up the leaf to form a neat package. Fill the remaining leaves in the same manner.

6. Return the bean mixture to a boil and place the romaine packages on top. Cover the pan and simmer for 8 minutes.

7. Season with salt and pepper to taste and serve immediately, garnished with scallion.

MENU 10

•

CHIPOTLE ROASTED
POTATOES

•

BAKED EGGS WITH
ESCAROLE, ONIONS,
AND GRUYÈRE

MARKET LIST

FRESH PRODUCE

2 pounds small red
   potatoes
1 medium onion
1 small bunch escarole
   (about 1 pound)
Garlic
Thyme
1 lemon

DAIRY

Unsalted butter
4 large eggs
8 ounces Gruyère

PANTRY

Extra-virgin olive oil
Cumin seeds
Chipotle chilis in adobo
   sauce
Sweet paprika
Coarse sea salt or
   kosher salt
Black peppercorns

EQUIPMENT

Large pot with lid
Large, heavy nonstick or
   cast-iron skillet
11 x 17-inch rimmed baking
   sheets
Steamer insert
Box grater
Wire whisk

MENU 10 GAME PLAN

1. Preheat the oven to
   450°F.
2. Prepare the chipotle
   roasted potatoes.
3. Prepare the baked eggs.
4. Serve wedges of the
   baked eggs with
   potatoes on the side.

CHIPOTLE ROASTED POTATOES

THIS IS ONE OF THOSE RECIPES THAT PUTS SPEED BEFORE EASE. STEAMING POTATOES BEFORE ROASTING THEM WILL REDUCE THE TOTAL COOKING TIME. HOWEVER, IT'S EASIER TO SIMPLY TOSS THE POTATOES IN RAW, EVEN IF IT DOES TAKE A LITTLE LONGER. IF YOU DO SKIP THE STEAMING STEP, ROAST THE POTATOES AT 400°F INSTEAD OF 450°F FOR ABOUT 45 MINUTES INSTEAD OF 15. EITHER WAY YOU'LL LOVE THE RESULTS, THOUGH BE FOREWARNED, THESE ARE SOME REALLY SPICY ROASTED POTATOES.

YIELD: 4 SERVINGS

2 pounds small red potatoes, halved
1 teaspoon cumin seeds
2 garlic cloves, peeled
2 teaspoons coarse sea salt or
    kosher salt
2 chipotle chilis in adobo sauce
⅓ cup extra-virgin olive oil
2 tablespoons freshly squeezed
    lemon juice
1 tablespoon fresh thyme leaves or
    1 teaspoon dried thyme
2 teaspoons sweet paprika

1. Preheat the oven to 450°F.

2. Add ½-inch of water to a large pot fitted with a steamer insert and bring to a boil. Add the potatoes and steam, covered, until barely tender, 8 to 10 minutes.

3. In a mortar, crush the cumin seeds. Add the garlic and salt and pound to a paste. Pound in the chipotles and a little of the adobo sauce. Stir in the oil, lemon juice, thyme leaves, and paprika. With a rubber spatula, scrape the mixture into a large bowl. Add the potatoes and stir to coat.

4. Transfer the potatoes to a rimmed baking sheet and roast until tender, about 15 minutes.

BAKED EGGS WITH ESCAROLE, ONIONS, AND GRUYÈRE

THIS DISH IS LIKE A FRITTATA, THOUGH FILLED WITH A HIGHER PROPORTION OF VEGETABLES THAN USUAL. OTHER GREENS THAT CAN BE SUBSTITUTED FOR THE ESCAROLE INCLUDE TENDER DANDELION, CHARD, OR BEET GREENS.

YIELD: **4** SERVINGS

2 tablespoons unsalted butter

1 medium onion, thinly sliced

Pinch of coarse sea salt or kosher
    salt, plus additional to taste

1 small bunch escarole (about
    1 pound), roughly chopped

4 large eggs

½ cup grated Gruyère cheese

Freshly milled black pepper

1. Preheat the oven to 450°F.

2. In a large, heavy nonstick or cast-iron skillet over high heat, melt the butter. Add the onion and a pinch of salt and sauté, stirring occasionally, until the onions soften, about 5 minutes.

3. In a large pot fitted with a steamer insert bring ½ inch of water to a boil. Add the escarole and steam, covered, until wilted, about 2 to 3 minutes. Transfer to the onion mixture and turn off the heat.

4. In a small bowl, whisk together the eggs, cheese, and salt and pepper to taste. Pour the egg mixture over the escarole mixture and stir to combine. Cook over high heat for about 1 minute, until the bottom begins to set. Transfer the pan to the oven and bake for 8 minutes. Turn on the broiler. Place the pan under the broiler, about 4 inches from the heat source, to brown the top, about 2 minutes. Serve immediately.

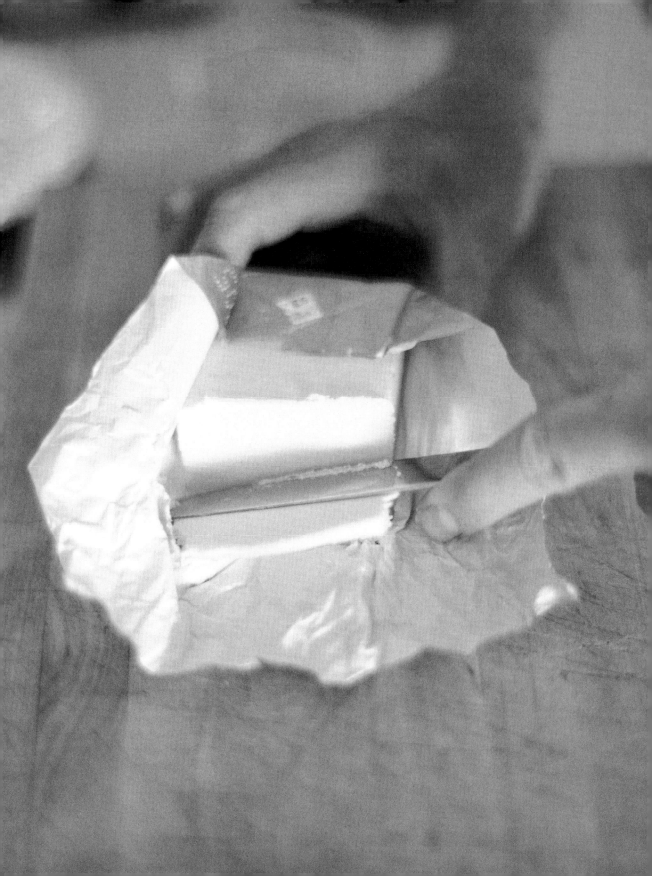

MENU 11

- BROCCOLI SALAD WITH GINGER VINAIGRETTE
- PAD THAI

MARKET LIST

FRESH PRODUCE

1 head romaine lettuce or 1 package romaine hearts
1 cup mung bean sprouts
1 large head broccoli
6 ounces fresh shiitake mushrooms
2 large carrots
1 bunch scallions
Garlic
Ginger
1 small bunch cilantro
1 lemon
1 lime

SOY

1 (8-ounce) package smoked tofu

PANTRY

Extra-virgin olive oil
Canola, peanut or light sesame oil
Rice vinegar
Soy sauce
Honey
Maple syrup
8 ounces rice noodles
Tabasco sauce or a favorite hot sauce
1 (14-ounce) can coconut milk (whole or light)
4 ounces roasted peanuts
Coarse sea salt or kosher salt
Black peppercorns
Mirin or sherry

EQUIPMENT

Large pot
Wok or large sauté pan
Large saucepan
Colander
Wire whisk
Citrus juicer

MENU 11 GAME PLAN

1. In a large pot, boil water for the broccoli and noodles.
2. Trim the broccoli.
3. Blanch the broccoli (reserve the water for the noodles).
4. Prepare the pad thai through step 1.
5. Finish the broccoli salad.
6. Finish the pad thai.
7. Serve the salad.
8. Serve the pad thai garnished with cilantro and lime.

BROCCOLI SALAD WITH GINGER VINAIGRETTE

IF YOU CAN FIND IT, TRY USING BROCCOLINI INSTEAD OF REGULAR BROCCOLI FLORETS. THE ENTIRE VEGETABLE IS EDIBLE, FROM THE SLENDER, ASPARAGUS-LIKE STALKS TO THE TINY FLORETS. IT'S CRUNCHY AND TENDER AT THE SAME TIME.

YIELD: **4** SERVINGS

2 tablespoons extra-virgin olive oil

1 tablespoon rice vinegar

1 tablespoon freshly squeezed lemon juice

1½ teaspoons grated fresh ginger

1 teaspoon soy sauce

¾ teaspoon honey

1 tablespoon coarse sea salt or kosher salt,
    plus additional to taste

Freshly milled black pepper

1 large head broccoli, florets separated,
    stalks peeled and sliced

1. In a salad bowl whisk together the oil, vinegar, lemon juice, ginger, soy sauce, honey, and salt and pepper to taste.

2. In a large saucepan, bring 2 quarts of water to a boil. Add the 1 tablespoon of salt and the broccoli and blanch until crisp-tender, about 2 minutes. Drain thoroughly and blot with a towel.

3. Add the broccoli to the vinaigrette and toss to combine. Season with salt and pepper. Serve immediately or refrigerate for 15 minutes.

PAD THAI

IF YOU THOUGHT THE ONLY WAY TO SATISFY YOUR PAD THAI CRAVING WAS TO ORDER IN, THINK AGAIN. WE USE SMOKED TOFU IN THIS RECIPE, BUT YOU CAN ALSO USE PLAIN EXTRA-FIRM TOFU.

YIELD: **4** SERVINGS

½ pound rice noodles

For the sauce
3 tablespoons soy sauce
2 tablespoons rice vinegar
2 tablespoons Tabasco or your
   favorite hot sauce
1 tablespoon mirin or sherry
1 tablespoon maple syrup or honey

For the vegetables and tofu
1 tablespoon canola, peanut, or light sesame oil
2 cups thinly sliced fresh shiitake mushrooms
1 cup coarsely grated carrot
1 bunch scallions, whites thinly sliced, greens
   cut into 1-inch pieces
1 garlic clove, finely chopped
½ pound smoked tofu, sliced into thin bite-sized
   strips (see Note)
1 (14-ounce) can coconut milk
2 cups shredded romaine lettuce
1 cup mung bean sprouts
½ cup roughly chopped roasted peanuts for garnish
1 small bunch cilantro, leaves and tender stems
   chopped, for garnish
1 lime, quartered, for garnish

1. Bring a large pot of water to a boil. Add the rice noodles and cook until barely tender, about 4 minutes. Drain, chill under cold running water, and drain again. Set aside.

2. To prepare the sauce, in a small bowl whisk together the soy sauce, vinegar, hot sauce, mirin, and maple syrup or honey.

3. In a wok or large sauté pan, heat the oil until it begins to smoke. Add the mushrooms, carrot, white part of the scallions, and garlic and stir-fry until the vegetables soften, about 2 to 3 minutes.

4. Add the sauce and the tofu and cook, stirring, until almost dry, about 4 minutes. Stir in the coconut milk and cook until the sauce reduces and begins to thicken, about 3 to 4 minutes.

5. Rinse the noodles briefly if they have begun to stick together. Drain and add to the vegetables.

6. Add the lettuce, bean sprouts, and peanuts and cook, stirring, for 1 to 2 minutes.

7. Serve immediately garnished with scallion greens, peanuts, cilantro, and lime wedges.

NOTE: SMOKED TOFU is exactly that; tofu that has usually been marinated in a soy mixture, and then flavored and firmed by smoking it. Look for it in the refrigerator case in Asian groceries and some health food stores.

MENU 12

·

BULGUR AND BUCKWHEAT PILAF

·

AUTUMN TEMPEH AND VEGETABLE STEW

MARKET LIST

FRESH PRODUCE
1½ pounds winter squash
1 large or 2 medium
    parsnips
2 large carrots
Scallions
2 medium onions
Garlic
Ginger
Rosemary or sage

DAIRY AND SOY
Unsalted butter
2 (8-ounce) packages soy
   tempeh

PANTRY
Extra-virgin olive oil
Soy sauce
Maple syrup
8 ounces coarse bulgur
   wheat
8 ounces whole toasted
   buckwheat groats
   (kasha)
4 (3- to 4-inch strips)
   kombu seaweed
Arrowroot powder
Coarse sea salt or kosher
   salt
Black peppercorns

EQUIPMENT
Medium Dutch oven
Heavy 2-quart pot with lid
Slotted spoon
Wire wisk
Kitchen shears for cutting
   Kombu

MENU 12 GAME PLAN
1. Adjust an oven rack to
   the middle of the oven
   and preheat the oven to
   400°F.
2. Prepare the stew through
   step 5.
3. Cook the bulgur.
4. Chop the scallions.
5. Finish the stew.
6. Serve the stew and grains
   together in wide soup
   plates and sprinkle with
   chopped scallions.

BULGUR AND BUCKWHEAT PILAF

THIS NUTTY, EARTHY PILAF IS A NICE CHANGE
OF PACE FROM RICE.

YIELD: **4** SERVINGS

2 tablespoons unsalted butter

**1 teaspoon coarse sea salt or
   kosher salt**

¾ cup coarse bulgur wheat

**¾ cup whole toasted buckwheat
   groats (kasha)**

1. In a heavy 2-quart saucepan over high heat, bring 3 cups of water to a boil and add the butter and salt.

2. Add the bulgur and buckwheat groats and return to a boil. Stir once, reduce the heat, and simmer the grains, covered, for 20 minutes. Fluff with a fork before serving.

AUTUMN TEMPEH AND VEGETABLE STEW

THIS IS A GREAT, WARMING DISH THAT TASTES AS IF IT HAS
SIMMERED ON THE STOVE FOR HOURS. LUCKILY, IT ONLY
TAKES ABOUT 30 MINUTES. THIN-SKINNED BUTTERCUP, RED
KURI, AND DELICATA ARE MY SQUASHES OF CHOICE, AND
THEY DO NOT REQUIRE PEELING.

YIELD: 4 SERVINGS

2 tablespoons unsalted butter

2 tablespoons extra-virgin olive oil

4 (3- to 4-inch) strips kombu
    seaweed, broken into 1-inch pieces

3 garlic cloves, chopped

1 tablespoon peeled, minced fresh
    ginger

2 sprigs fresh rosemary or sage

2 (8-ounce) packages tempeh, cut into
    1-inch squares

4 tablespoons soy sauce

1 tablespoon maple syrup

2 medium onions, cut into ½-inch-thick slices

1½ pounds winter squash, seeded and cut
    into 2-inch chunks

1 large or 2 medium parsnips, peeled and cut
    into ½-inch-thick slices

2 large carrots, peeled and cut into
    ½-inch-thick slices

Coarse sea salt or kosher salt

2 teaspoons arrowroot powder

2 scallions, thinly sliced

1. Preheat the oven to 400°F.

2. In a medium Dutch oven over medium heat, melt the butter with the oil. Add the kombu and sauté for 2 minutes. Add the garlic, ginger, and rosemary or sage. Arrange the tempeh in a layer on top.

3. In a small bowl, whisk 1 cup of water with 2 tablespoons of the soy sauce with the maple syrup. Pour over the tempeh.

4. Top the tempeh with a layer each of onions, squash, parsnip, and carrot, in that order, and sprinkle with salt. Cover the casserole and bring to a boil.

5. Transfer the casserole to the oven and bake until the vegetables are tender, about 25 minutes.

6. With a slotted spoon, transfer the vegetables and tempeh to a serving bowl. Drain back any juices into the casserole and place over medium heat.

7. In a small bowl, dissolve the arrowroot in 1 ½ cups of cold water and the remaining 2 tablespoons soy sauce and whisk into the juices. Simmer, stirring constantly, until the sauce thickens.

8. Pour the sauce over the tempeh and vegetables. Gently fold in the scallions and serve immediately with the pilaf.

AUTUMN

Honey-Roasted Pears

Roasted Grapes with Red Wine

New Crop Assorted Nuts Roasted
in the Shell with Dried Fruits

Fresh Fig Crostini with Ricotta
and Honey on Toasted Walnut Bread

Prunes in Red Wine and Rosemary Syrup

Maple Chestnut Mousse

Apples with Honey and Cinnamon

Whole Meal Biscuits
with Cheeses and Grapes

DESSERTS

HONEY-ROASTED PEARS

COMICE PEARS WORK WELL IN THIS RECIPE, BUT YOU CAN
SUBSTITUTE ANOTHER VARIETY OF RIPE PEAR.

YIELD: **4** SERVINGS

4 ripe Comice pears, quartered
   lengthwise and cored
3 tablespoons cold unsalted butter, cut into ½-inch cubes
¼ cup clover honey
1 teaspoon vanilla extract

1. Preheat the oven to 450°F.

2. Place the pears in a large, heavy skillet or enamel-lined cast-iron gratin dish.

3. Drizzle with honey and dot with butter. Sprinkle the vanilla over the pears and set the pan over high heat for 2 minutes. Transfer the pan to the oven and roast for 15 minutes.

ROASTED GRAPES WITH RED WINE

MOST PEOPLE DON'T THINK TO ROAST GRAPES. BUT THEY
SHOULD, SINCE ROASTING CONDENSES AND CARAMELIZES
THEIR JUICES. IT'S A GREAT TECHNIQUE.

YIELD: **4** SERVINGS

2 tablespoons unsalted butter
1 pound red seedless grapes, stemmed
2 tablespoons brown sugar, preferably Demerara (see page 8)
⅓ cup dry red wine (any red wine you like to drink will do)
1 pint vanilla ice cream for serving

1. Preheat the oven to 425°F and place a baking dish in the oven.

2. Add the butter to the preheated baking dish and let it melt. Add the grapes and sugar and stir to coat.

3. Roast the grapes for 10 minutes. Add the wine to the pan and roast for 15 minutes more. Serve warm, with vanilla ice cream.

NEW CROP ASSORTED NUTS ROASTED IN THE SHELL WITH DRIED FRUITS

MY MOM ALWAYS HAD NUTS IN THEIR SHELLS AND AN ASSORTMENT OF DRIED FRUITS ON HAND FOR IMPROMPTU DESSERTS AND SNACKS. ROASTING THE NUTS IN THEIR SHELLS MAKES THEM SWEETER AND "NUTTIER." MAKE SURE YOU SELECT FINE, FRESH NUTS AND MOIST FRUITS.

YIELD: **4** SERVINGS

1 pound assorted nuts in the shell, such as almonds, hazelnuts, walnuts, and pecans
1 pound assorted dried fruits, such as figs, apricots, pears, peaches, and apples

1. Set a rack in the middle shelf of the oven and preheat to 400°F.

2. Spread the nuts on a rimmed baking sheet and roast for 30 minutes.

3. Transfer the nuts to a bowl to cool. Crack open while still warm and serve with dried fruits and a good sherry.

FRESH FIG CROSTINI WITH RICOTTA AND HONEY ON TOASTED WALNUT BREAD

FOR A RICHER DESSERT, SUBSTITUTE SLICES OF POUND CAKE.

YIELD: **4** SERVINGS

2 tablespoons unsalted butter
8 thin slices walnut bread
8 ounces fresh whole-milk ricotta cheese
8 large fresh Mission figs, sliced, for serving
½ cup honey for drizzling

1. In a large heavy skillet over medium heat, melt the butter. Add the bread slices and turn them over in the butter. Cook until lightly browned and crisp, about 3 minutes per side, regulating the heat to prevent the bread from burning. Transfer the bread to a rack to cool.

2. Bring the bread, ricotta, figs, and honey to the table and let each diner assemble their own crostini.

PRUNES IN RED WINE AND ROSEMARY SYRUP

CHOOSE LARGE PLUMP PRUNES WITH THEIR PITS—THEY HOLD
THEIR SHAPE BETTER THAN PITTED ONES, AND THEY MAKE
THE DISH MORE FUN TO EAT.

YIELD: **4** TO **6** SERVINGS

1 pound large, unpitted prunes
1 cup dry red wine
⅔ cup honey
1 sprig fresh rosemary
3 strips fresh lemon zest
Vanilla ice cream or crème fraîche
　　for serving
Chopped lightly toasted nuts, such as almonds,
　　pecans, or walnuts, for garnish (see page 7)

1. In a pressure cooker over high heat, combine 1 cup of water with the prunes, wine, honey, rosemary, and lemon zest. Lock the lid in place and bring to full pressure. Reduce the heat to low and cook for 5 minutes.

2. Transfer the pot to the sink and run cold water over it to release the pressure. Transfer the prunes with their juice to a serving bowl and let cool slightly. Serve warm, with vanilla ice cream or crème fraîche and chopped nuts.

MAPLE CHESTNUT MOUSSE

YOU CAN FIND COOKED CANNED OR JARRED
CHESTNUTS IN GOURMET STORES AND SUPERMARKETS,
ESPECIALLY AROUND THANKSGIVING.

YIELD: **4** SERVINGS

1 cup heavy cream
1 (12-ounce) jar whole unsweetened cooked
 chestnuts (about 1½ cups)
½ cup maple syrup
½ teaspoon vanilla extract
Tiny pinch of fine sea salt
Grated bittersweet chocolate for garnish

1. Pour ¾ cup of the cream into a metal bowl. Refrigerate until cold.

2. In the bowl of a food processor fitted with a metal blade, process the chestnuts, maple syrup, vanilla, and salt and until smooth. Add the remaining ¼ cup of cream and process again until well combined.

3. Remove the bowl of cream from the refrigerator and whip until soft peaks form.

4. Serve the mousse topped with a dollop of whipped cream and a sprinkle of grated chocolate.

APPLES WITH HONEY
AND CINNAMON

YIELD: **4** SERVINGS

4 crisp, tart apples, such as Pink Lady, Macoun,
 Granny Smith, or McIntosh, cored and sliced into wedges
1 cup raw honey for drizzling
Ground cinnamon for sprinkling

Arrange the apples on a platter and serve with honey and cinnamon.

WHOLE MEAL BISCUITS WITH CHEESES AND GRAPES

THESE CRISP, SLIGHTLY SWEET BISCUITS ARE
PERFECT WITH ANY TYPE OF CHEESE.

YIELD: **18** TO **20** BISCUITS

1 cup rolled oats
¾ cup whole wheat pastry flour, plus
    additional for rolling
1 tablespoon brown sugar, preferably
    Demerara (see page 8)
½ teaspoon baking soda
½ teaspoon salt
⅛ teaspoon freshly milled black pepper
5 tablespoons cold unsalted butter,
    cut into cubes
⅓ cup whole-milk yogurt
Cheese for serving
Grapes for serving

1. Preheat the oven to 400°F. Line a rimmed baking sheet with parchment paper.

2. In the bowl of a food processor, process the oats, flour, sugar, baking soda, salt, and pepper for 8 to 10 seconds, to form a meal. Add the butter and pulse 8 times to combine. Add the yogurt and pulse a few times. The dough will be fairly dry, but should just hold together.

3. Transfer the dough to a lightly floured surface and roll it out to ⅛-inch thickness. Cut into rounds with a 2-inch cookie cutter and transfer to the prepared pan. Re-roll any scraps and repeat.

4. Prick each biscuit several times with the tines of a fork. Bake until lightly browned, about 12 to 15 minutes. Rotate the pans after about 7 minutes for even baking. Cool slightly on a wire rack. Arrange the biscuits on a platter with a cool cluster of grapes and 1 or more cheeses at room temperature, such as Morbier, Brie, or blue.

Rest. . . . We descend into the darkness of a watery world; the surface of things is slick and glistening. All energy flows deep within the ground, to the roots. In heavy pots and casseroles we simmer hearty stews and compotes to comfort and warm us. We cling to the hearth, and the sweet fragrances of cinnamon, nutmeg, and clove scent our dreams. We find our roots in music and books, and the chill of starlight illuminates the ice. Turnips, carrots, burdock, parsnips, and beets caramelize to earthy-brown sweetness. Buckwheat, kasha, and beans fortify against the cold and damp. And the salty edge of aged miso and cheese strengthens and thickens our blood.

WINTER

WINTER MENUS

1. **Sautéed Kale with Red Cabbage and Caraway Seeds**
   Porcini Mushroom and Parsley Risotto

2. **Sautéed Broccoli with Lemon and Garlic**
   Whole Grain Pasta with Red Wine, Red Bean, and Portobello Ragout

3. **Spicy Coconut Sweet Potato Soup with Collard Greens**
   Crispy Tempeh Strips
   Jasmine Rice

4. **Balsamic-Roasted Seitan with Cipollini Onions**
   Garlic Mashed Potatoes and Parsnips
   Crunchy Cabbage Salad

5. **Warm White Bean Salad with Sun-Dried Tomatoes and Smoked Mozzarella**
   Provençal Garlic and Herb Broth

6. **Leek and Potato Frittata**
   Romaine Salad with Red Wine Vinaigrette and Asiago Toasts

7. Green Apple and Celery Salad with Walnuts and Mustard Vinaigrette
Kasha Casserole with Root Vegetables and Mushrooms

8. Watercress and Radicchio Salad
Hot Open-Faced Tempeh Sandwich with Mushroom Gravy
Maple-Roasted Carrots

9. Lemon Lentil Soup with Spinach
Buckwheat Vegetable Pancakes with Spicy Yogurt Sauce

10. Tomato Goat Cheese Strata
Broccoli Rabe with Balsamic Brown Butter

11. Grilled Gruyère and Red Onion Sandwiches with Grainy Mustard
Leek and Turnip Soup with Potatoes and Chard

12. Toasted Millet Pilaf
Winter Vegetable Stew with Maple-Glazed Tofu

MENU 1

•

SAUTÉED KALE WITH RED CABBAGE AND CARAWAY SEEDS

•

PORCINI MUSHROOM AND PARSLEY RISOTTO

MARKET LIST

FRESH PRODUCE
1 bunch kale (about 14 ounces)
1 red cabbage
1 medium onion
Garlic
Thyme
Flat-leaf parsley

DAIRY
Unsalted butter
4 ounces Parmesan cheese

PANTRY
½ ounce dried porcini mushrooms (about ½ cup)
Extra-virgin olive oil
Apple cider vinegar
Caraway seeds
8 ounces Carnaroli or Arborio rice
Coarse sea salt or kosher salt
Black peppercorns

EQUIPMENT
Large saucepan with lid
Pressure cooker
Fine-mesh strainer
Salad spinner

MENU 1 GAME PLAN
1. Prepare the risotto through step 1.
2. Chop the onions and garlic for the risotto and greens.
3. Prep the kale and cabbage.
4. Cook the risotto through step 3.
5. Cook the kale and cabbage.
6. Wash and chop the parsley, and grate the cheese.
7. Finish the risotto.
8. Serve the risotto with the kale and cabbage on the side.

SAUTÉED KALE WITH RED CABBAGE AND CARAWAY SEEDS

NOT ONLY DOES KALE SURVIVE FREEZING TEMPERATURES, IT ACTUALLY HITS ITS PEAK DURING THE COLDEST MONTHS OF THE YEAR. COLD WEATHER CONCENTRATES THE CARBOHYDRATES WITHIN THE LEAVES, YIELDING A SWEETER FLAVOR. LOOK FOR REALLY TIGHT CURLY LEAVES RATHER THAN THE FLAT, FLABBY KIND.

YIELD: **4** SERVINGS

2 tablespoons extra-virgin olive oil
2 garlic cloves, sliced
¾ teaspoon caraway seeds
2 cups thinly sliced red cabbage
1 bunch kale (about 14 ounces), washed
    leaves stripped from their stems and
    roughly chopped
½ teaspoon coarse sea salt or kosher salt,
    plus additional to taste
Apple cider vinegar
Freshly milled black pepper

1. In a large saucepan over medium heat, warm the oil. Add the garlic and caraway seeds and sauté for 30 seconds. Add the cabbage and cook, stirring occasionally, for 2 minutes. Add the kale, ¼ cup of water, and ½ teaspoon of salt. Cover the pot and cook over high heat until the kale and cabbage are tender, about 5 to 7 minutes.

2. Season with vinegar, salt, and pepper and serve hot.

PORCINI MUSHROOM AND PARSLEY RISOTTO

THE QUICKEST WAY TO REHYDRATE DRIED FOODS IS TO SOAK THEM IN BOILING WATER. REHYDRATED DRIED MUSHROOMS HAVE A MORE CONCENTRATED FLAVOR THAN FRESH, SO THEY GIVE FORTH A BIG, EARTHY TASTE. WHEN PURCHASING DRIED PORCINI, TRY TO FIND WHOLE MUSHROOMS RATHER THAN LITTLE PIECES; THEY ARE LIKELY TO BE OF BETTER QUALITY. A POPULAR GARNISH, PARSLEY IS FEATURED HERE AS A MAJOR INGREDIENT. PARSLEY IS AN HERB WORTH COOKING, ESPECIALLY THE MORE ROBUST FLAT-LEAF VARIETY. IT'S IMPORTANT TO REMOVE THE TOUGH STEMS, WHICH YOU CAN USE FOR MAKING BROTH LATER. OR, IF YOU HAVE THE TIME, TRY SIMMERING THE PARSLEY STEMS IN THE PORCINI SOAKING LIQUID FOR A FEW MINUTES BEFORE STRAINING.

YIELD: 4 SERVINGS

½ ounce dried porcini mushrooms
    (about ½ cup)
2 tablespoons extra-virgin olive oil
1 cup diced onion (about 1 medium)
½ teaspoon coarse sea salt or kosher salt
1 cup Carnaroli or Arborio rice
2 garlic cloves, finely chopped
3 sprigs fresh thyme
½ cup firmly packed chopped fresh
    flat-leaf parsley
⅓ cup grated Parmesan cheese, plus
    additional for serving
2 tablespoons unsalted butter
Freshly milled black pepper

1. In a small bowl, cover the mushrooms with 2 cups of boiling water and set aside until soft, about 7 to 10 minutes. Rub the mushrooms between your fingers to dislodge any grit at the bottom of the bowl. Remove the mushrooms from the liquid and chop them coarsely. Strain the liquid through a fine-mesh strainer into a small bowl, stopping short of the grit at the bottom of the bowl. Add enough water to equal 3 cups liquid.

2. In a pressure cooker over medium heat, warm the oil. Add the onion and salt and sauté for 2 minutes. Raise the heat and add the rice, mushrooms, garlic, and thyme. Cook for 1 more minute, stirring.

3. Add the mushroom water and bring to a boil. Lock the lid in place and bring to full pressure. Reduce the heat to low and cook for 7 minutes. Transfer the pot to the sink and run under cold water to release the pressure. Remove the lid and return the pot to the stove. Pick out the thyme branches.

4. Add the parsley and cook, stirring, over medium heat for 1 minute, or until the rice thickens. Stir in the cheese and butter. Season with salt and pepper and serve immediately with additional grated Parmesan.

HOW TO WASH PARSLEY

Fill the bowl of your salad spinner with water and, holding the whole bunch by the stems, invert it in the water and swish the leaves around to remove all the grit. Then pluck the leaves from the stems, spin them dry, and chop. I like to use up any leftover parsley leaves in a salad while they're still nice and fresh.

MENU 2

•

SAUTÉED BROCCOLI WITH LEMON AND GARLIC

•

WHOLE GRAIN PASTA WITH RED WINE, RED BEAN, AND PORTOBELLO RAGOUT

MARKET LIST

FRESH PRODUCE
1 large head broccoli
2 large portobello mushrooms
1 large red onion
Garlic
Sage
1 lemon
Flat-leaf parsley or cilantro

DAIRY
4 ounces Gruyère cheese

PANTRY
Extra-virgin olive oil
Soy sauce
12 ounces whole wheat penne, rigatoni, or fusilli
Hot paprika
1 (14-ounce) can whole peeled tomatoes packed in juice
1 (15-ounce) can red kidney beans
Coarse sea salt or kosher salt
Black peppercorns
Dry red wine

EQUIPMENT
Large pot with lid
Large sauté pan
Large skillet
Colander
Box grater

MENU 2 GAME PLAN
1. Boil water in a large pot for the broccoli and pasta.
2. Prepare the ragout ingredients, and slice extra garlic for the broccoli.
3. Cook the ragout.
4. Prep the broccoli.
5. Salt the boiling water and cook the broccoli through step 1, reserving the water for the pasta.
6. Cook the pasta.
7. Finish the broccoli
8. Chop the parsley, grate the Gruyère , and slice a lemon into wedges for garnish.
9. Drain the pasta and toss with ragout. Serve the broccoli on the side.

SAUTÉED BROCCOLI WITH LEMON AND GARLIC

ONE OF THE REASONS FOR FEATURING THESE TWO DISHES TOGETHER IS THAT YOU SAVE TIME BY ONLY HAVING TO BOIL ONE POT OF WATER. YOU COOK THE BROCCOLI FIRST, AND THEN COOK THE PASTA IN THE BROCCOLI WATER.

YIELD: **4** SERVINGS

2 tablespoons coarse sea salt or kosher salt
1 large head broccoli, separated into florets,
    stems peeled and sliced
2 tablespoons extra-virgin olive oil
2 garlic cloves, thinly sliced
Freshly milled black pepper
Lemon wedges for serving

1. Fill a large pot with water, cover and bring it to a boil over high heat. Add salt and broccoli and cook, uncovered, until crisp-tender, about 2 to 3 minutes. Drain well.

2. In a large skillet over medium heat, warm the oil. Add the garlic and cook for 30 seconds. Add the blanched broccoli, season with salt and pepper, and sauté for 5 minutes.

3. Serve with lemon wedges.

WHOLE GRAIN PASTA WITH RED WINE, RED BEAN, AND PORTOBELLO RAGOUT

ANY NICE, CHUNKY PASTA WORKS WELL WITH THIS HEARTY, RIB-STICKING RAGOUT. HOWEVER, IF YOU'RE NOT IN THE MOOD FOR PASTA, YOU CAN SERVE THE RAGOUT AS A STEW, ACCOMPANIED BY BREAD OR RICE, OR MAKE IT INTO A SOUP BY THINNING IT WITH A LITTLE WATER OR VEGETABLE STOCK.

YIELD: **4** SERVINGS

For the pasta
Coarse sea salt or kosher salt
12 ounces whole wheat penne, rigatoni, or fusilli

For the ragout
2 tablespoons extra-virgin olive oil
1 cup diced red onion
4 garlic cloves, thinly sliced
7 fresh sage leaves, chopped
2 large portobello mushrooms,
    stems removed, caps sliced
    into 1-inch pieces
1 teaspoon hot paprika
½ cup dry red wine
1 (14-ounce) can whole peeled tomatoes with
    their juice, coarsely chopped
1 (15-ounce) can red kidney beans
2 teaspoons soy sauce
¼ cup grated Gruyère cheese for garnish
2 tablespoons chopped fresh parsley or
    cilantro for garnish

1. Fill a large pot with water, bring it to a boil, and add 2 tablespoons salt.

2. Meanwhile, in a large sauté pan over medium heat, warm the oil until hot, but not smoking. Add the onion, garlic, sage, and 1 teaspoon of salt and sauté, stirring occasionally, for 2 minutes.

3. Raise the heat and add the mushrooms and paprika. Sauté until the mushrooms soften, about 2 minutes.

4. Add the pasta to the pot of boiling water and stir once with a wooden spoon. Cook until al dente, and drain.

5. Add the wine to the pan with the ragout, scrape up the brown bits from the bottom of the pan with a wooden spoon, and bring to a boil. Continue boiling until slightly thickened, about 2 minutes.

6. Add the tomatoes with their juice, beans with their liquid, and soy sauce. Reduce the heat to medium and simmer, uncovered, until the liquid has reduced to a rich sauce, about 10 minutes.

7. Serve the pasta topped with the ragout and sprinkled with Gruyère and parsley.

MENU 3

•

SPICY COCONUT SWEET POTATO SOUP WITH COLLARD GREENS

•

CRISPY TEMPEH STRIPS

•

JASMINE RICE

MARKET LIST

FRESH PRODUCE
1 bunch collard greens
    (about 14 ounces)
1 small jalapeño pepper
1 large sweet potato
1 large or 2 medium
    onions
Ginger
Garlic
1 bunch cilantro
1 lime

DAIRY
Unsalted butter
2 (8-ounce) packages
    soy tempeh

PANTRY
Extra-virgin olive oil
1 pint neutral oil, such as
    canola, grapeseed, or
    sunflower oil
Coriander seeds
Turmeric
1 pound white
    jasmine rice
1 (14-ounce) can
    unsweetened
    coconut milk
Coarse sea salt or
    kosher salt

EQUIPMENT
Large sauté pan or skillet
Large saucepan with lid
Medium saucepan with lid

MENU 3 GAME PLAN
1. Make the rice.
2. Prepare the soup through
   step 2.
3. Prepare the collard
   greens and cilantro.
4. Fry the tempeh and drain
   and season it.
5. Finish the soup.
6. Slice the lime.
7. Serve the soup.

SPICY COCONUT SWEET POTATO SOUP WITH COLLARD GREENS

WITH ALL ITS DIVERSE COMPONENTS, THIS COMPLEX SOUP IS REALLY A COMFORTING ONE-DISH MEAL. WHILE IT'S GREAT SERVED WITH JASMINE RICE, YOU CAN ALSO SERVE IT WITH FLATBREAD OR CORNBREAD.

YIELD: 4 SERVINGS

2 tablespoons extra-virgin olive oil

2 cups diced onion (about 2 medium)

2 teaspoons coarse sea salt or kosher salt, plus additional to taste

1 large sweet potato, peeled and
    cut into 1-inch chunks (about 4 cups)

3 garlic cloves, finely chopped

1 small jalapeño pepper with seeds, minced

1 tablespoon minced fresh ginger

1 teaspoon coriander seeds, toasted and ground
    (see page 8), or 1 teaspoon ground coriander

½ teaspoon turmeric

1 (14-ounce) can coconut milk

1 small bunch collard greens, tough stems
    removed, and leaves cut in half along the rib,
    and then crosswise into ¼-inch-wide strips

1 lime, cut into wedges

½ cup roughly chopped cilantro, for garnish

1. In a large saucepan over medium heat, warm the oil. Add the onion and a pinch of salt, and sauté until softened, for 3 to 4 minutes.

2. Add the sweet potato, garlic, jalapeño, ginger, coriander, and turmeric, and sauté for 2 minutes. Add 2 cups of water, the coconut milk, and 2 teaspoons of salt, raise the heat, and bring to a boil. Reduce the heat and simmer, covered, for 15 minutes.

3. Add the collard greens to the soup and simmer, uncovered, until tender, about 10 minutes. Add a bit of water if the soup is too thick.

4. Ladle the soup into 4 wide soup plates, and top with a spoonful of jasmine rice and several crispy tempeh strips. Squeeze lime over all and sprinkle with cilantro.

CRISPY TEMPEH STRIPS

TEMPEH IS TRADITIONALLY FRIED, GIVING IT THAT GOOD CRISPY TEXTURE THAT CONTRASTS NICELY IN THIS CREAMY SOUP. IT'S IMPORTANT TO SEASON THE TEMPEH AS SOON AS IT'S DONE FRYING BECAUSE YOU WANT THE SALT TO BE ABSORBED IMMEDIATELY.

YIELD: **4** SERVINGS

2 (8 ounce) packages soy tempeh, cut into 3 x ¼-inch strips
2 cups neutral oil, such as canola, sunflower, or grapeseed oil
Coarse sea salt or kosher salt

In a large sauté pan over medium heat, warm the oil until hot but not smoking. Fry the tempeh in batches (don't crowd the pan) until golden-brown, about 3 to 4 minutes. Drain on paper towels and sprinkle with salt.

SOMETHING EXTRA: JASMINE RICE

THE CHEWY TEXTURE OF JASMINE RICE REALLY STANDS UP TO THE TEMPEH.

YIELD: **4** SERVINGS

2 cups jasmine rice, rinsed
1 tablespoon unsalted butter (optional)
1 teaspoon coarse sea salt or kosher salt

1. In a medium saucepan over high heat, combine the rice, butter if desired, and salt with 3 cups of water, and bring to a boil. Stir the rice once, reduce the heat, and cover the pan.

2. Cook until the water is absorbed and the rice begins to stick on the bottom, about 18 to 20 minutes. Turn off the heat and let sit, covered, for 5 minutes. Uncover, fluff with a fork, and serve.

MENU 4

•

BALSAMIC-ROASTED SEITAN WITH CIPOLLINI ONIONS

•

GARLIC MASHED POTATOES AND PARSNIPS

•

CRUNCHY CABBAGE SALAD

MARKET LIST

FRESH PRODUCE
1 small head green
   cabbage
1 pound parsnips
1 ½ pounds potatoes
   (red or Yukon gold)
1 ½ pounds cipollini
   onions
1 head garlic
Rosemary
Flat-leaf parsley

DAIRY AND PERISHABLES
Unsalted butter
2 (8-ounce) packages
   seitan

PANTRY
Extra-virgin olive oil
Apple cider vinegar
Balsamic vinegar
Soy sauce
Brown sugar, preferably
   Demerara (see page 8)
Honey
2 ounces shelled walnuts
   (optional)
Coarse sea salt or
   kosher salt
Black peppercorns
Dry red wine, such as
   Côtes du Rhone, Chianti,
   or Cabernet

EQUIPMENT
Small ovenproof skillet
10-inch ovenproof sauté
   pan or 3-quart brazier
Two large saucepans
Colander or sieve
Potato masher
Wire whisk

MENU 4 GAME PLAN
1. Preheat oven to 350°F.
2. Prepare the cabbage
   salad through step 2.
3. Raise the oven
   temperature to 475°F.
4. Prepare the seitan and
   onions through step 2.
5. Prepare the cabbage
   through step 4.
6. Finish the seitan.
7. Prepare the garlic
   mashed potatoes, if
   desired.
8. Finish the salad.
9. Chop the parsley.
10. Serve the seitan and
    onions over the mashed
    potatoes and parsnips,
    if desired, with cabbage
    salad on the side.
    Garnish with chopped
    parsley.

BALSAMIC-ROASTED SEITAN WITH CIPOLLINI ONIONS

LOOK FOR BIG CIPOLLINI ONIONS FOR THIS RECIPE, BECAUSE THE LARGER THEY ARE, THE FASTER IT IS TO PEEL THEM. IF YOU CAN'T GET CIPOLLINI ONIONS, YOU CAN USE LARGE SHALLOTS INSTEAD. MAKE SURE YOU LEAVE THE ROOT ENDS ON SO THAT THE ONIONS DON'T FALL APART. SEITAN IS A GOOD INGREDIENT TO HAVE ON HAND. IT FREEZES WELL, DOESN'T LOSE ITS TEXTURE, KEEPS FOR MONTHS, AND DEFROSTS QUICKLY. I HIGHLY RECOMMEND THAT YOU MAKE THE MASHED POTATOES AND PARSNIPS (PAGE 235) TO ACCOMPANY THIS DISH. IT REALLY WORKS WELLS WITH ALL THE FLAVORS. BUT IF YOU DON'T HAVE TIME, SERVE THE SEITAN WITH COUNTRY BREAD OR RICE.

YIELD: **4** SERVINGS

1½ pounds cipollini onions
2 (8 ounce) packages seitan, cut
    into 1-inch chunks
2 sprigs fresh rosemary
1 cup dry red wine
⅓ cup balsamic vinegar
¼ cup extra-virgin olive oil
¼ cup soy sauce
1 tablespoon honey
1 tablespoon chopped fresh parsley

1. Preheat the oven to 475°F.

2. In a large saucepan over high heat, bring 4 cups of water to a boil. Add the onions and blanch for 30 seconds. Drain the onions in a sieve or colander and cool under cold running water. Pull off their skins and drain.

3. In a large ovenproof sauté pan or 3-quart brazier, arrange the onions in a single layer. Add the seitan and rosemary.

4. In a small bowl, whisk together the wine, vinegar, oil, soy sauce, and honey with ⅓ cup of water. Pour the mixture evenly over the onions and seitan, place the pan over high heat, and bring to a boil.

5. Transfer the pan to the oven and roast the seitan and onions for 25 minutes, stirring occasionally for even browning.

6. Serve over mashed potatoes and parsnips, if desired, and garnish with parsley.

SOMETHING EXTRA:
GARLIC MASHED POTATOES AND PARSNIPS

THE COOKING WATER IN THIS RECIPE CAN BE SAVED, FROZEN FOR UP TO 3 MONTHS, AND USED AS THE BASE FOR A FLAVORFUL SOUP STOCK. TRY IT IN THE LEMON LENTIL SOUP WITH SPINACH (PAGE 257), LEEK AND TURNIP SOUP (PAGE 268), OR WINTER VEGETABLE STEW WITH MAPLE-GLAZED TOFU (PAGE 272).

YIELD: 4 SERVINGS

1½ pounds potatoes (such as red or
    Yukon gold), cut into chunks
1 pound parsnips, peeled and cut into chunks
1½ tablespoons coarse sea salt or
    kosher salt, plus additional to taste
1 head garlic, cloves separated and peeled
¼ cup (½ stick) unsalted butter or
    extra-virgin olive oil
Freshly milled black pepper

1. Put the potatoes, parsnips, and peeled garlic cloves in a large saucepan with 6 cups of water. Bring to a boil and add the salt. Reduce the heat and simmer until the vegetables mash easily when pressed against the side of the pan with a wooden spoon, about 15 minutes.

2. Set aside ½ cup of the cooking water. Drain the potatoes and parsnips and return them to the saucepan. Add the butter or oil and mash to the consistency you prefer. Add a little of the reserved cooking water if the mashed vegetables are too thick. Season with salt and pepper and serve.

CRUNCHY CABBAGE SALAD

THIS SIMPLE, REFRESHING WINTER SALAD NICELY OFFSETS
THE RICHNESS OF THE OTHER DISHES.

YIELD: **4** SERVINGS

1 small head green cabbage, quartered and
   cut crosswise into thin strips (about 6 cups)
1 teaspoon coarse sea salt or kosher salt
¼ cup apple cider vinegar
2 tablespoons extra-virgin olive oil
1 teaspoon sugar, preferably organic washed
   cane sugar (see page 8)
Freshly milled black pepper
⅓ cup minced fresh parsley
¼ cup walnuts, coarsely chopped (optional)

1. Preheat the oven to 350°F.

2. In a large bowl, toss the cabbage with the salt and squeeze gently with your hands until the cabbage begins to exude some juice.

3. Spread out the walnuts in a small skillet or pan and toast in the oven for 8 minutes.

4. In a small bowl, whisk together the vinegar, oil, and sugar.

5. Pour the dressing over the cabbage and toss to combine. Season with pepper. Add the parsley and toss again. Chill the salad for 20 minutes before serving.

6. Add the toasted walnuts to the chilled salad, toss, and serve.

MENU 5

•

WARM WHITE BEAN SALAD WITH SUN-DRIED TOMATOES AND SMOKED MOZZARELLA

•

PROVENÇAL GARLIC AND HERB BROTH

MARKET LIST

FRESH PRODUCE
2 bunches arugula
Celery
2 medium carrots
1 medium red onion
1 head garlic
Sage
Thyme
Rosemary
Flat-leaf parsley
1 orange

DAIRY
2 large eggs
4 ounces Parmesan cheese
8 ounces smoked mozzarella

PANTRY
Extra-virgin olive oil
Red wine vinegar
Bay leaves
Crushed red pepper flakes
1 (15-ounce) can white beans
4 ounces sun-dried tomatoes (not oil-packed)
Coarse sea salt or kosher salt
Black peppercorns
1 loaf country bread

EQUIPMENT
Large sauté pan with lid
2 medium saucepans, one with lid
Salad spinner
Mesh strainer
Box grater
Wire whisk

MENU 5 GAME PLAN
1. Prepare the broth through step 1.
2. Soften the dried tomatoes in boiling water if necessary.
3. Prepare the white bean salad through step 3.
4. Toast the bread and rub it with garlic.
5. Finish the broth.
6. Grate the cheese for the broth and chop the parsley for both dishes.
7. Rinse and dry the arugula and toss it with the white beans.
8. Serve the soup and salad.

WARM WHITE BEAN SALAD WITH SUN-DRIED TOMATOES AND SMOKED MOZZARELLA

THIS IS A TRUE WINTER SALAD—WARM AND SAVORY. THE SMOKED MOZZARELLA REALLY ADDS ANOTHER LAYER OF FLAVOR, BUT YOU CAN USE REGULAR MOZZARELLA IF YOU LIKE. IF YOUR TOMATOES ARE VERY DRY, SOAK THEM IN VERY HOT WATER TO COVER UNTIL SUPPLE.

YIELD: 4 SERVINGS

½ cup firmly packed sun-dried tomatoes
  (not oil-packed, see page 165)
½ cup extra-virgin olive oil
1 cup diced red onion (about 1 medium)
½ teaspoon coarse sea salt or kosher
  salt, plus additional to taste
1 cup thinly sliced peeled carrots
  (about 2 medium)
1 cup thinly sliced celery stalks (about 2 medium)
2 garlic cloves, minced
2 tablespoons finely chopped fresh rosemary
½ teaspoon crushed red pepper flakes
1 (15-ounce) can white beans, drained
¼ cup red wine vinegar
½ pound smoked mozzarella, diced
4 cups arugula leaves, for serving
2 tablespoons finely chopped fresh flat-leaf
  parsley for garnish

1. In a large sauté pan over high heat, combine the oil, onion, and ½ teaspoon of salt and sauté for 2 minutes. Add the carrots, celery, garlic, rosemary, and red pepper flakes and sauté for 1 more minute. Add ¼ cup of water and cover the pan. Cook over high heat until the vegetables are just crisp-tender, about 2 minutes.

2. Uncover the pan and turn off the heat. Stir in the beans, tomatoes, mozzarella, and vinegar, and season with salt.

3. Toss the beans with the arugula and serve garnished with chopped parsley.

PROVENÇAL GARLIC AND HERB BROTH

A PUNGENT BROTH MADE FROM PLENTY OF GARLIC AND HERBS IS A TRADITIONAL HANGOVER CURE IN SOUTHERN FRANCE AND SPAIN. IT'S A VERY QUICK AND SIMPLE BROTH TO MAKE. HERE, TO MAKE IT MORE SUBSTANTIAL, I ENRICH IT WITH EGG AND SERVE IT OVER CROUTONS WITH GRATED PARMESAN CHEESE.

YIELD: 4 SERVINGS

4 garlic cloves, peeled and halved
    lengthwise
4 fresh sage leaves
2 (2-inch) strips orange zest
1 sprig fresh thyme
1 bay leaf
2 large eggs
1 tablespoon extra-virgin olive oil
Coarse sea salt or kosher salt and
    freshly milled black pepper
4 slices country bread, toasted and rubbed with garlic
¼ cup grated Parmesan cheese for garnish
2 tablespoons minced fresh parsley for garnish

1. In a medium saucepan over high heat, combine 5 cups of water, garlic, sage, orange zest, thyme, and bay leaf and bring to a boil. Cover the pan, reduce the heat to low, and simmer for 15 minutes.

2. Meanwhile, in a small bowl, combine the eggs and oil, beating lightly with a fork.

3. Strain the broth and discard the solids. Return the broth to the saucepan and bring to a simmer.

4. Whisk ¼ cup of the broth into the egg mixture to warm it. Transfer the egg mixture to the saucepan and heat gently until the soup thickens, about 1 to 2 minutes. Season with salt and pepper.

5. Place a slice of toasted bread in each of 4 serving bowls. Ladle the soup over the bread and sprinkle with cheese and parsley. Serve immediately.

MENU 6

-

LEEK AND
POTATO FRITTATA

-

ROMAINE SALAD WITH
RED WINE VINAIGRETTE
AND ASIAGO TOASTS

MARKET LIST

FRESH PRODUCE

2 heads romaine lettuce
1 pound small red or
    white potatoes
3 medium leeks
1 small shallot
Thyme
Flat-leaf parsley

DAIRY

6 large eggs
4 ounces Asiago cheese

PANTRY

Extra-virgin olive oil
Red wine vinegar
Dijon-style mustard
Sugar, preferably
    organic washed cane
    sugar (see page 8)
Coarse sea salt or
    kosher salt
1 loaf country bread
Black peppercorns

EQUIPMENT

Large ovenproof skillet
Medium saucepan with lid
Rimmed baking sheet
Salad spinner
Wire whisk

MENU 6 GAME PLAN

1. Preheat the oven to
   400°F and prepare the
   frittata through step 3.
2. Prepare the frittata
   through step 3.
3. Prepare the salad
   dressing.
4. Bake the frittata.
5. Wash the salad greens
   and spin them dry.
6. Chop the parsley.
7. Prepare the Asiago
   toasts.
8. Toss the salad.
9. Slice the frittata and
   serve straight from the
   skillet, with salad and
   Asiago toasts.

LEEK AND POTATO FRITTATA

TRADITIONALLY, A FRITTATA IS COOKED ENTIRELY ON THE
STOVE TOP IN A SKILLET, AND INVERTED HALFWAY THROUGH
SO THAT IT COOKS ON BOTH SIDES. HERE, YOU'RE MAKING A
BAKED FRITTATA—IT STARTS OUT ON THE STOVE TOP, BUT
FINISHES UP IN THE OVEN, A TECHNIQUE THAT IS NOT ONLY
EASIER BUT INSURES EVEN COOKING AS WELL.

YIELD: 4 TO 6 SERVINGS

¼ cup extra-virgin olive oil
3 medium leeks, white and tender
    green parts only, cleaned
    (see page 61), and thinly sliced (3 cups)
3 teaspoons coarse sea salt or
    kosher salt
1 tablespoon finely chopped
    fresh thyme leaves
1 pound small red or white potatoes, scrubbed
    and thinly sliced (about 3 cups)
6 large eggs
Freshly milled black pepper
1 tablespoon minced fresh parsley for garnish

1. Set a rack on the middle shelf of the oven and preheat to 400°F.

2. In a large ovenproof skillet over high heat, warm the oil. Add the leeks and 2 teaspoons of salt and sauté until softened and lightly browned, about 3 minutes. Lower the heat, add the thyme, cover, and cook for 10 minutes.

3. Meanwhile, place the potatoes in a medium saucepan with enough water to cover by ½ inch. Cook over medium heat, covered, until the potatoes are tender, but not falling apart, 8 to 10 minutes. Drain and transfer to the skillet.

4. In a medium bowl, whisk together the eggs and the remaining teaspoon of salt. Season with black pepper. Add the eggs to the skillet and stir to combine. Transfer the pan to the oven and bake until firm and slightly puffed, about 20 minutes.

5. Sprinkle with parsley, cut into wedges, and serve hot or warm.

ROMAINE SALAD WITH RED WINE VINAIGRETTE AND ASIAGO TOASTS

SINCE ROMAINE HEADS CAN VARY IN SIZE AND YIELD, AFTER TRIMMING AWAY OUTER LEAVES THAT MAY BE LESS THAN PERFECT, I RECOMMEND FOUR CUPS TORN LEAVES (LOOSELY PACKED) PER SERVING AS A GUIDE. YOU CAN ALSO SUBSTITUTE OTHER GREENS HERE, SUCH AS PREWASHED MESCLUN, BUT THE ROMAINE HAS A GREAT CRUNCH THAT IS VERY REFRESHING IN THE WINTER.

YIELD: **4** SERVINGS

2 tablespoons red wine vinegar
1 small shallot, peeled and finely chopped
Pinch of sugar, preferably organic
   washed cane sugar (see page 8)
Pinch of coarse sea salt or kosher salt
4 thick slices country bread
¼ pound Asiago cheese, coarsely grated
2 teaspoons Dijon-style mustard
6 tablespoons extra-virgin olive oil
Freshly milled black pepper
2 heads romaine lettuce, trimmed,
   washed, spun dry, and torn into
   bite-size pieces

1. Preheat the oven to 400°F. In a large salad bowl, combine the vinegar, shallot, sugar, and salt. Set aside for 5 minutes or so while you prepare the toasts.

2. Arrange the bread on a rimmed baking sheet. Toast until lightly browned, about 5 minutes. Remove from the oven and light the broiler.

3. Mound the Asiago onto the pieces of toast. Broil the bread 4 inches from the heat source until the cheese is bubbling, about 3 to 4 minutes.

4. Meanwhile, whisk first the mustard and then the oil into the vinegar mixture. Season with black pepper.

5. Toss the greens with the vinaigrette and serve with cheese toasts.

MENU 7

•

**GREEN APPLE
AND CELERY SALAD
WITH WALNUTS AND
MUSTARD VINAIGRETTE**

•

**KASHA
CASSEROLE WITH
ROOT VEGETABLES
AND MUSHROOMS**

MARKET LIST

FRESH PRODUCE

1 bunch celery
   (with leaves)
3 large portobello
   mushrooms
2 medium parsnips
2 medium carrots
Scallions
Garlic
2 medium onions
Flat-leaf parsley
1 lemon
1 large Granny Smith
   apple

PANTRY

Extra-virgin olive oil
Dijon-style mustard
Coriander seeds
Fennel seeds
Caraway seeds
Honey
8 ounces whole
   kernel kasha
1 (15-ounce) can
   chickpeas
3 ounces walnuts
Coarse sea salt or
   kosher salt
Black peppercorns

EQUIPMENT

Dutch oven
Small skillet
Kettle or small saucepan
Salad spinner (optional)
Wire whisk
Citrus juicer
Spice mill, clean coffee
   grinder, or mortar pestle

MENU 7 GAME PLAN

1. Prepare the casserole.
2. Prepare the salad.
3. Slice the scallions and
   chop the parsley for the
   casserole.
4. Serve the salad.
5. Serve the casserole,
   garnished with scallion
   and parsley.

GREEN APPLE AND CELERY SALAD WITH WALNUTS AND MUSTARD VINAIGRETTE

THIS SALAD IS ALL ABOUT THE NUANCE OF CRUNCH. THE
GREEN APPLE, CELERY, AND WALNUT EACH HAVE A
DIFFERENT YET COMPLEMENTARY TOOTHSOME QUALITY IN
THE MOUTH. IT'S A GREAT WINTER SALAD.

YIELD: **4** SERVINGS

6 large or 8 medium celery stalks
⅓ cup roughly chopped walnuts
2 tablespoons freshly squeezed
  lemon juice
2 tablespoons Dijon-style mustard
1 garlic clove, crushed
2 teaspoons honey
½ teaspoon coarse sea salt or kosher salt
5 tablespoons extra-virgin olive oil
Freshly milled black pepper
1 large Granny Smith apple
¼ cup minced celery leaves

1. Peel away and discard any tough fibers from the celery stalks. Trim the celery leaves and reserve. Cut the celery on the bias into ⅛-inch-thick pieces about 1 inch in length. Transfer the celery pieces to a bowl of cold water and refrigerate.

2. In a small skillet over medium heat, toast the nuts for 3 to 4 minutes, shaking the pan for even browning. Transfer to a plate to cool.

3. In a salad bowl, combine the lemon juice, mustard, garlic, honey, and salt. Whisk in the oil and season with pepper.

4. Peel and quarter the apple. Core and cut each quarter into 2 wedges. Cut the wedges crosswise into thin slices. Add the apple slices to the dressing and toss.

5. Drain the chilled celery and dry in a salad spinner or blot dry with a paper towel.

6. Add the celery, celery leaves, and walnuts to the apples and toss. Serve immediately or refrigerate for up to 1 hour.

KASHA CASSEROLE WITH ROOT VEGETABLES AND MUSHROOMS

KASHA AND MUSHROOMS HAVE AN AFFINITY FOR EACH OTHER; BOTH ARE TENDER AND SOFT, AND THE MUSHROOMS ADD SOME GLAMOUR AND BRIGHTNESS TO THE HEARTY GRAIN. THIS COMFORTING DISH REMINDS ME OF KASHA *VARNISHKES* (AN EASTERN EUROPEAN KASHA AND NOODLE DISH), BUT WITH ROOT VEGETABLES INSTEAD OF NOODLES.

YIELD: **6** SERVINGS

1 teaspoon coriander seeds
½ teaspoon fennel seeds
½ teaspoon caraway seeds
½ teaspoon black peppercorns
¼ cup extra-virgin olive oil
2 medium onions, chopped
3 large portobello mushrooms,
    stemmed, caps cut into ½-inch cubes
2 medium parsnips, peeled and thinly sliced
2 medium carrots, peeled and thinly sliced
1 (15-ounce) can chickpeas, drained
1 cup whole-kernel kasha
1 tablespoon coarse sea salt or kosher salt
¼ cup minced fresh flat-leaf parsley for garnish
2 scallions, thinly sliced, for garnish

1. In a kettle or small saucepan, bring 4 cups of water to a boil. Put the coriander, fennel, caraway, and peppercorns in a spice mill, clean electric coffee grinder, or mortar and grind to a powder.

2. Warm a Dutch oven over high heat for 30 seconds. Add the oil, onions, and ground spices and sauté for 2 minutes. Add the mushrooms and sauté for 1 more minute, stirring. Add the parsnips and carrots and sauté for 2 more minutes. Add the boiling water, chickpeas, kasha, and salt. When the mixture returns to a boil, lower the heat, cover the pot, and simmer until the kasha is tender, about 25 minutes.

3. Serve immediately, garnished with parsley and scallions.

MENU 8

• • •

WATERCRESS AND RADICCHIO SALAD

• • •

HOT OPEN-FACED TEMPEH SANDWICH WITH MUSHROOM GRAVY

• • •

MAPLE-ROASTED CARROTS

MARKET LIST

FRESH PRODUCE
2 bunches watercress
1 large head radicchio
6 ounces cremini mushrooms
2 pounds carrots
1 medium onion
Garlic
Sage
2 lemons

DAIRY AND SOY
Unsalted butter
2 (8 ounce) packages soy tempeh

PANTRY
Extra-virgin olive oil
Soy sauce
Maple syrup
All-purpose flour
Coarse sea salt or kosher salt
Black peppercorns
1 loaf country bread

EQUIPMENT
Medium pot
Large sauté pan
Rimmed baking sheet
Steamer insert
Salad spinner
Wire whisk
Citrus juicer

MENU 8 GAME PLAN
1. Place a baking pan on the middle shelf of the oven and preheat the oven to 450°F.
2. Steam the carrots, if desired.
3. Prepare the salad dressing.
4. Roast the carrots.
5. Prepare the tempeh.
6. Wash and dry the salad greens.
7. Toast the bread.
8. Toss the salad.
9. Serve the tempeh and gravy over toast, with carrots and salad on the side.

WATERCRESS AND RADICCHIO SALAD

RADICCHIO IS GREAT FOR QUICK SALADS BECAUSE IT'S ALREADY PRETTY CLEAN, AND THE TIGHT HEADS JUST NEED A RINSE BEFORE BEING TORN INTO PIECES. IT'S ALSO PRETTY, WITH BRIGHT MAGENTA LEAVES.

YIELD: 4 SERVINGS

½ garlic clove
2 ½ tablespoons freshly squeezed
    lemon juice
½ teaspoon coarse sea salt or
    kosher salt
⅓ cup extra-virgin olive oil
Freshly milled black pepper
2 bunches watercress, trimmed
1 large head radicchio, leaves
    separated and torn (about 2 cups)

1. Vigorously rub the inside of a salad bowl with the garlic.

2. Add the lemon juice and salt to the bowl and stir to dissolve. Whisk in the oil and season with pepper. Toss the watercress and radicchio with the dressing and serve.

HOT OPEN-FACED TEMPEH SANDWICH WITH MUSHROOM GRAVY

I PUT THIS SANDWICH ON THE MENU WHEN I WAS THE CHEF AT ANGELICA KITCHEN IN NEW YORK CITY. IT WAS SO POPULAR THAT I HAD TO THINK OF A WAY IT COULD BE MADE IN THE HOME KITCHEN. TO THAT END, I'VE ADAPTED THE RECIPE SO THAT EVERYTHING HAPPENS IN ONE PAN.

YIELD: **4** SERVINGS

1 cup thinly sliced onion (about
    1 medium onion)
2 cups thinly sliced cremini
    mushrooms (6 ounce mushrooms)
¼ cup extra-virgin olive oil
1 garlic clove, finely chopped
1 tablespoon finely chopped fresh sage
2 (8 ounce) packages soy tempeh,
    cut into 1 x 3-inch strips
3 tablespoons all-purpose flour
¼ cup soy sauce
Sliced and toasted country bread, for serving
2 tablespoons minced fresh parsley for garnish

1. In a large sauté pan over high heat, warm the oil. Add the onion to cook, stirring occasionally, until lightly browned, about 2 minutes. Add the mushrooms, oil, garlic, and sage and cook for 1 minute.

2. Stir in the tempeh and flour and cook for 3 minutes. (The flour will begin to stick to the pan.)

3. Add 3 cups of water and the soy sauce. Scrape up the flour and vegetables from the bottom of the pan.

4. Bring the mixture to a boil. Reduce the heat and simmer until the sauce thickens and the tempeh is cooked through, about 5 to 7 minutes.

5. Spoon the tempeh and mushroom gravy over the toasted bread and sprinkle with chopped parsley. Serve hot, with roasted carrots and salad on the side.

MAPLE-ROASTED CARROTS

REMEMBER, TO SHORTEN THE ROASTING TIME OF ANY ROOT VEGETABLE, YOU CAN PRESTEAM IT. FOR EVEN SPEEDIER COOKING, YOU CAN USE BAGGED BABY CARROTS.

YIELD: 4 SERVINGS

2 pounds carrots, peeled and cut on the bias into 1-inch pieces ½ inch thick

3 tablespoons maple syrup

1 tablespoon lemon juice

1 tablespoon unsalted butter or extra-virgin olive oil

½ teaspoon coarse sea or kosher salt

1. Set an oven rack on the middle shelf and preheat to 475°F.

2. Pour ½ inch of water into a pot fitted with a steamer insert and bring to a boil over high heat. Add the carrots, cover and steam for 5 minutes.

3. Place a rimmed baking sheet or baking dish (it should be large enough to hold the carrots in a single layer) in the oven to heat.

4. In a large bowl, combine the maple syrup, lemon juice, butter, and salt.

5. Drain the carrots well, transfer them to the bowl, and toss to coat. With a rubber spatula scrape the carrots onto the baking sheet and roast, stirring halfway through the cooking time, until tender and lightly caramelized, about 15 minutes.

MENU 9

•

LEMON LENTIL SOUP WITH SPINACH

•

BUCKWHEAT VEGETABLE PANCAKES WITH SPICY YOGURT SAUCE

MARKET LIST

FRESH PRODUCE
1 (10 ounces) pre-
    washed baby spinach
1 small head green
    cabbage
3 medium carrots
1 bunch scallions
1 head garlic
Ginger
Rosemary
Dill
Cilantro
1 lemon

DAIRY
Unsalted butter
    (if using)
4 eggs
1 quart whole-milk
16 ounces whole-milk
    yogurt

PANTRY
Neutral oil such, as
    grapeseed, canola, or
    sunflower
Extra-virgin olive oil
Cayenne pepper
1 bay leaf
All-purpose flour
Buckwheat flour
Baking powder
12 ounces red lentils
1 (14-ounce) can
    chopped tomatoes
    packed in juice

Coarse sea salt or
    kosher salt
Black peppercorns

EQUIPMENT
Large sauté pan or
    skillet (or 2 small ones)
Pressure cooker
Rimmed baking sheet
Wire whisk
Citrus juicer
Cheese cloth
Kitchen string

MENU 9 GAME PLAN
1. Preheat the oven to
   250°F.
2. Prepare the yogurt sauce
   and chill.
3. Prepare the soup through
   step 2.
4. Prepare the pancakes.
5. Finish the soup.
6. Serve the soup.
7. Serve the pancakes with
   yogurt sauce.

LEMON LENTIL SOUP
WITH SPINACH

FRESH LEMON ADDS A WONDERFUL BRIGHT TONE TO THIS
LENTIL SOUP. PRESSURE COOKING THE BROWN LENTILS IS
JUST ABOUT AS FAST AS OPENING A CAN, AND YOU GET
MUCH TASTIER RESULTS. USING PREWASHED BAGS OF BABY
SPINACH ELIMINATES THE HASSLE OF TRIMMING AND WASHING.

YIELD: 4 SERVINGS

1½ cups red or brown lentils, rinsed
1 cup canned chopped tomatoes
    with their juice
3 tablespoons extra-virgin olive oil
8 garlic cloves, peeled
2 teaspoons coarse sea salt or
    kosher salt
4 slices peeled fresh ginger, each
    about the size of a quarter
1 sprig fresh rosemary
1 bay leaf
1 (10 ounces) bag washed baby spinach
2 tablespoons freshly squeezed lemon juice
Freshly milled black pepper

1. In a pressure cooker over high heat, combine 5 cups of water with the lentils, tomatoes, oil, garlic, and salt. Wrap the ginger, rosemary, and bay leaf in a piece of cheesecloth, tie it closed with kitchen string, and add this bouquet garni to the pot. Lock the lid in place and bring to full pressure. Reduce the heat to low and simmer for 10 minutes.

2. Transfer the pressure cooker to the sink and run cold water over it to release the pressure. Remove the lid and discard the bouquet garni.

3. Return the pot to medium heat. Add the spinach and simmer until wilted. Stir in the lemon juice. Crush the garlic against the side of the pot with the back of a spoon and stir so that all the garlic completely melts into the soup. Add pepper and serve immediately.

BUCKWHEAT VEGETABLE PANCAKES WITH SPICY YOGURT SAUCE

THIS RECIPE IS DERIVED FROM AN ASIAN PANCAKE THAT I LEARNED HOW TO MAKE AT MY VERY FIRST RESTAURANT JOB. THAT ONE WAS MADE WITH WHEAT FLOUR, BUT HERE I USE BUCKWHEAT FLOUR. THERE ARE TWO TYPES OF BUCKWHEAT FLOUR: WHAT YOU TYPICALLY FIND IN AMERICAN HEALTH FOOD STORES IS WHOLE (DARK) BUCKWHEAT FLOUR, WHICH CONTAINS THE SEED COAT AND HAS A DISTINCTIVE GRAY COLOR. LIGHTER BUCKWHEAT FLOUR IS HARDER TO FIND. YOU CAN USE EITHER HERE. BUCKWHEAT FLOUR GOES RANCID QUICKLY, SO BE SURE TO STORE IT IN YOUR FREEZER, WHERE IT WILL KEEP FOR EIGHT TO TEN MONTHS.

YIELD: 4 SERVINGS

For the yogurt sauce
2 cups whole-milk yogurt
⅓ cup chopped fresh cilantro
1 garlic clove, minced
1 teaspoon coarse sea salt or kosher salt
¼ teaspoon cayenne pepper, or to taste

For the pancakes
2 cups all-purpose flour
1 cup buckwheat flour
2½ teaspoons coarse sea salt or kosher salt
2 teaspoons baking powder
3 cups whole-milk
4 large eggs
2 tablespoons melted butter or neutral oil, such as grapeseed, canola, or sunflower
3 cups shredded green cabbage (1 small head)
1½ cups shredded peeled carrot (about 3 medium carrots)
6 scallions, white and tender green parts only, thinly sliced
2 tablespoons chopped fresh dill
¼ cup neutral oil, for frying, such as grapeseed, canola, or sunflower
Fresh cilantro sprigs for garnish

1. Preheat the oven to 250°F.

2. To prepare the yogurt sauce, in a small bowl, stir together all the ingredients until well combined. Chill until ready to serve.

3. To make the pancake batter, in a large bowl, whisk together the flours, salt, and baking powder. In a separate bowl, whisk together the milk, eggs, and butter or oil. Pour the wet mixture over the dry and stir to combine.

4. Add the cabbage, carrots, scallions, and dill to the batter and mix well. The batter will be thick.

5. In a large (or 2 small) sauté pan(s) or skillet(s) over medium heat, warm ¼ cup of oil. When the oil is hot, pour a scant cup of batter into the pan to form a pancake and fry for 5 minutes. Flip the pancakes and fry for 5 minutes more. As you finish each pancake, transfer it to a rimmed baking sheet and keep warm in the oven.

6. Transfer the pancakes to a clean cutting surface and cut each one into 4 wedges. Arrange 4 to 6 wedges on each of 4 plates. Pour yogurt sauce on top and garnish with cilantro sprigs.

MENU 10

•

TOMATO GOAT CHEESE STRATA

•

BROCCOLI RABE WITH BALSAMIC BROWN BUTTER

MARKET LIST

FRESH PRODUCE
2 bunches broccoli rabe
1 medium onion
Flat-leaf parsley
Sage
Garlic

DAIRY
Unsalted butter
6 large eggs
8 ounces heavy cream
4 ounces fresh goat
    cheese
4 ounces Parmesan or
    Grana Padano cheese

PANTRY
Extra-virgin olive oil
Balsamic vinegar
Crushed red pepper
    flakes
1 (28-ounce) can diced
    tomatoes packed in juice
Coarse sea salt or
    kosher salt
Black peppercorns
½ pound day-old
    artisanal bread

EQUIPMENT
Large pot
Large ovenproof
    sauté pan
Small skillet
Box grater
Wire whisk

MENU 10 GAME PLAN

1. Set an oven rack on the middle shelf of the oven and preheat to 450°F.
2. Bring a large pot of water to a boil for the broccoli rabe, and maintain it at a simmer.
3. Prepare the strata.
4. Prepare the brown butter sauce.
5. Boil and drain the broccoli rabe.
6. Toss the broccoli rabe with the sauce and season with salt and pepper.
7. Serve the strata with broccoli rabe on the side.

TOMATO GOAT CHEESE STRATA

I LIKE TO DESCRIBE THIS DISH, ONE OF MY FAVORITES, AS A
SAVORY BREAD PUDDING WITH CHEESE.

YIELD: **4** SERVINGS

6 large eggs
1 cup heavy cream
3 tablespoons minced fresh
   flat-leaf parsley
1 medium onion, thinly sliced
2 tablespoons extra-virgin olive oil
2 large garlic cloves, roughly chopped
1 tablespoon minced fresh sage
½ teaspoon crushed red pepper flakes
1 (28-ounce) can diced tomatoes with their juice
1 teaspoon coarse sea salt or kosher salt
½ pound day-old artisanal bread, cut into 1-inch cubes (about 6 cups)
¼ pound fresh goat cheese
¼ cup freshly grated Parmesan or Grana Padano cheese

1. Set a rack on the middle shelf of the oven and preheat to 450°F.

2. In a medium bowl, whisk together the eggs, cream, and parsley and set aside.

3. Place a 10-inch, ovenproof sauté pan or 3-quart brazier over high heat. When the pan is hot, add the onions. Cook until lightly browned, about 2 minutes. Add the oil, garlic, sage, and red pepper flakes and sauté, stirring, for 1 more minute. Add the tomatoes and salt and bring to a simmer.

4. Stir the bread into the tomatoes. Crumble the goat cheese over the bread, then pour the egg and cream mixture over all and sprinkle with the Parmesan cheese. Bake until the strata has set and is golden on top, about 25 minutes. Lest rest for 5 minutes before serving.

BROCCOLI RABE WITH BALSAMIC BROWN BUTTER

IF YOU THINK YOU DON'T LIKE BROCCOLI RABE, NOW'S THE TIME TO GIVE IT ANOTHER CHANCE. THESE DAYS YOU'RE LIKELY TO FIND MILDER VARIETIES. HERE I'VE PAIRED IT WITH A FRAGRANT BROWN BUTTER. WHEN YOU WARM BUTTER, THE MILK SOLIDS SEPARATE AND SINK TO THE BOTTOM, TURNING HAZELNUT BROWN AND TAKING ON A REALLY NUTTY FLAVOR. THE RICHNESS OF THE BUTTER IS THEN CUT WITH BALSAMIC VINEGAR. YOU CAN ALSO USE ANY INTERESTING TYPE OF VINEGAR, SUCH AS SHERRY OR HERB VINEGAR, OR EVEN LEMON OR OTHER CITRUS JUICE. TRY THIS SAUCE OVER OTHER VEGETABLES, SUCH AS BRUSSELS SPROUTS, BROCCOLI, CAULIFLOWER, OR KALE.

YIELD: **4** SERVINGS

6 tablespoons unsalted butter

3 tablespoons balsamic vinegar

2 bunches broccoli rabe, trimmed

2 tablespoons coarse sea salt or kosher salt

1. Bring a large pot of water to a boil.

2. Melt the butter in a small skillet over high heat. Let it cook until the white solids sink to the bottom and turn a light brown (you will no longer hear a sizzling sound), about 5 minutes. Stir in the vinegar and cook 30 seconds. Remove the pan from the heat.

3. Add the broccoli rabe and salt to the boiling water. Boil the broccoli rabe uncovered, for 2 minutes, then drain well.

4. Transfer the broccoli rabe to a bowl and toss with the balsamic butter. Serve immediately.

MENU 11

•

GRILLED GRUYÈRE AND RED ONION SANDWICHES WITH GRAINY MUSTARD

•

LEEK AND TURNIP SOUP WITH POTATOES AND CHARD

MARKET LIST

FRESH PRODUCE

1 bunch Swiss chard
1 pound small white
  turnips
1 pound small red
  potatoes
2 medium leeks
4 medium red onions
Garlic

DAIRY

Unsalted butter
8 ounces Gruyère cheese

PANTRY

Extra-virgin olive oil
Caraway seeds
Whole grain mustard
Crisp kosher pickles
Coarse sea salt or
  kosher salt
Black peppercorns
1 loaf country sourdough
  bread, preferably with
  some rye in it

EQUIPMENT

Large saucepan or
  pot with lid
Very large skillet
Large sieve
Slotted spoon or tongs

MENU 11 GAME PLAN

1. Prepare the soup through
   step 2.
2. Make the sandwiches.
3. Add the greens and
   finish the soup.
4. Accompany the soup and
   sandwiches with some
   crisp kosher dill pickles.

GRILLED GRUYÈRE AND RED ONION SANDWICHES WITH GRAINY MUSTARD

THE KEY TO MAKING THESE PRESSED SANDWICHES, OR PANINI, IS USING GREAT BREAD. I SUGGEST A FRESH ARTISANAL RYE BREAD. ALSO, YOU'LL FIND THAT A GOOD QUALITY GRUYÈRE FROM A GOURMET CHEESE STORE IS FAR SUPERIOR TO ANY PREPACKAGED CHEESE.

YIELD: **4** SERVINGS

3 tablespoons unsalted butter
3 tablespoons extra-virgin olive oil
4 medium red onions, sliced into ¼-inch-thick rings (about 4 cups)
8 slices country sourdough bread, preferably with some rye in it
Whole grain mustard, for spreading
½ pound Gruyère cheese, thinly sliced

1. In a very large skillet over medium heat, melt the butter and add the oil (or use 2 skillets, dividing the ingredients between them). Add the onions and sauté until golden, about 5 to 7 minutes. Remove the skillet from the heat.

2. Hold a large sieve over the skillet(s). Use a slotted spoon or a pair of tongs to transfer the onions to the sieve. Let the onion-flavored butter and oil mixture drip back into the pan and transfer the onions to a plate.

3. Spread each piece of bread with mustard and divide the onions among 4 of the slices. Top the onions with cheese slices and place a slice of bread on top to form 4 sandwiches.

4. Return the skillet to medium heat and add the sandwiches, in batches if necessary (add a bit more oil if the pan gets dry between batches). Place a skillet or large plate over the sandwiches and put a heavy object on top. Fry the sandwiches until the cheese has melted and the bread is golden brown, about 3 minutes per side. Drain the sandwiches on paper towels, then transfer them to a cutting board and cut in half. Serve immediately.

LEEK AND TURNIP SOUP WITH POTATOES AND CHARD

LIKE CUMIN AND FENNEL, CARAWAY HELPS US DIGEST
SULFUROUS VEGETABLES SUCH AS TURNIPS. IF YOU BUY
TURNIPS WITH THE GREEN TOPS STILL ON, TRY SUBSTITUTING
THEM FOR THE SWISS CHARD.

YIELD: **4** TO **6** SERVINGS

3 tablespoons unsalted butter

2 medium leeks, white and tender green
   parts only, cleaned (see page 61)
   and thinly sliced

1 teaspoon coarse sea salt or
   salt, plus additional to taste

4 garlic cloves, chopped

1 tablespoon caraway seeds

1 pound small white turnips, cut into
   ¾-inch pieces

1 pound small red potatoes, cut into
   1-inch pieces

1 bunch Swiss chard, trimmed and leaves
   roughly chopped

Freshly milled black pepper

1. In a large saucepan over medium heat, melt the butter. Add the leeks, season with a little salt, and sauté until soft, about 3 minutes. Add the garlic and caraway seeds and sauté for 1 more minute.

2. Add 6 cups of water, the turnips, and potatoes, and bring to a boil over high heat. Add the 1 teaspoon of salt, reduce the heat to medium, and simmer, covered, until the vegetables are tender, about 10 to 15 minutes.

3. Add the chard and simmer until wilted, 2 to 3 more minutes. Season with salt and plenty of pepper and serve immediately.

MENU 12

•

TOASTED MILLET PILAF

•

WINTER VEGETABLE STEW WITH MAPLE-GLAZED TOFU

MARKET LIST

FRESH PRODUCE

2 to 3 heads baby bok
  choy (about ¾ pound
  total)
1 pound winter squash
1 fennel bulb
2 medium turnips
2 medium carrots
Scallions
1 large onion
Garlic
Ginger

DAIRY

1 ½ pounds extra-firm
  tofu

PANTRY

Extra-virgin olive oil
Soy sauce
Crushed red pepper
  flakes
Maple syrup
12 ounces millet
Coarse sea salt or
  kosher salt

EQUIPMENT

Large sauté pan with lid
Large skillet
Medium saucepan with
  lid
Pressure cooker
Wire whisk

MENU 12 GAME PLAN

1. Bring the water to a boil
   for the millet and add the
   oil and salt.
2. Toast the millet.
3. Press the tofu.
4. Cook the millet.
5. Prepare the stew through
   step 6.
6. Cook the tofu.
7. Finish the stew.
8. Slice the scallion.
9. Serve the stew.

TOASTED MILLET PILAF

TOASTED MILLET IS MORE FLAVORFUL AND QUICKER TO
COOK THAN UNTOASTED MILLET.

YIELD: **4** SERVINGS

1 tablespoon extra-virgin olive oil
½ teaspoon coarse sea salt or kosher salt
1½ cups millet

1. In a medium saucepan, bring 2¾ cups of water to a boil and add the oil and salt.

2. Meanwhile, in a large skillet over medium heat, toast the millet for 5 minutes, stirring and shaking the pan frequently for even toasting.

3. Carefully add the hot millet to the boiling water and cover. Reduce the heat and simmer for 20 minutes. Turn off the heat and allow the millet to sit, covered, for 5 minutes. Fluff with a fork and serve.

WINTER VEGETABLE STEW WITH MAPLE-GLAZED TOFU

ALL OF MY FAVORITE WINTER VEGETABLES APPEAR IN THIS
STEW. IF YOU LIKE, YOU CAN DOUBLE THE TOFU PART OF THIS
RECIPE AND USE IT LATER IN A QUICK SANDWICH OR WRAP.

YIELD: **4** SERVINGS

For the tofu
1 ½ pounds extra-firm tofu, drained
5 tablespoons soy sauce
3 tablespoons extra-virgin olive oil
3 tablespoons maple syrup
3 garlic cloves, sliced
1 teaspoon crushed red pepper flakes

For the stew
2 tablespoons extra-virgin olive oil
1 large onion, cut into chunks
2 medium turnips, peeled and cut into chunks
2 medium carrots, peeled and cut into
    1-inch pieces
1 pound winter squash, peeled, seeded and
    cut into 8 wedges or chunks
1 fennel bulb, trimmed and cut into chunks
1 tablespoon chopped fresh ginger
2 ½ teaspoons coarse sea salt or kosher salt
2 or 3 heads baby bok choy (about ¾ pound
    total), cut into large pieces
Chopped fresh scallions for garnish

1. To prepare the tofu, wrap it in a clean kitchen towel and press gently but firmly to extract excess water. Cut the tofu into 8 slices.

2. In a large sauté pan, arrange the tofu in a single layer.

3. In a small bowl, whisk together the soy sauce, oil, maple syrup, garlic, and red pepper flakes and pour over the tofu.

4. Bring the mixture to a boil over high heat. Reduce the heat to medium, cover, and cook for 4 minutes. Flip the pieces and cook, uncovered, until almost dry, about 4 to 5 minutes.

5. To prepare the stew, in a pressure cooker over high heat, warm the oil. Add the onion and sauté until softened and lightly browned, about 3 minutes. Add 3 cups of water and bring to a boil. Add the turnips, carrots, squash, fennel, ginger, and salt. Lock the lid in place and bring to full pressure. Reduce the heat and simmer for 4 minutes.

6. Transfer the pressure cooker to the sink and run under cold water to release the pressure. Remove the lid and return the pot to high heat. The vegetables should be perfectly tender; if they are not, continue simmering the stew, uncovered, over medium heat until done.

7. Add the bok choy and simmer for 1 minute, until bright green and tender. Stir in the glazed tofu.

8. Serve the stew over millet pilaf, sprinkled with the scallions.

WINTER

Broiled Pineapple with
Honey, Ginger, and Lime

Sautéed Apples with Raisins
and Brown Sugar

Chocolate Fondue

Caramelized Bananas with
Blood Orange and Pistachio

Apricots in Spiced Honey-Wine Syrup

Apple Cider Couscous Cake
with Red Currant Glaze

Grapefruit Cocktail with Mascarpone
and Toasted Almonds

DESSERTS

BROILED PINEAPPLE WITH HONEY, GINGER, AND LIME

SWEET CARAMELIZED PINEAPPLE IS A REAL TREAT IN WINTER, WHEN YOU NEED SOMETHING BRIGHT AND JUICY TO BREAK THE MONOTONY.

YIELD: **4** SERVINGS

½ ripe pineapple, peeled, quartered lengthwise
into wedges, and cored
4 tablespoons (½ stick) unsalted butter,
cut into 8 pieces
½ cup honey
1 tablespoon freshly squeezed lime juice
1 tablespoon finely chopped fresh ginger
1 tablespoon brown sugar, preferably Demerara
(see page 8)

1. Preheat the broiler to low and set an oven rack 4 inches from the heat source.

2. Slice the pineapple wedges across into ½-inch-thick pieces. Spread the pineapple in a baking dish and dot with butter.

3. In a small bowl, stir together the honey, lime juice, and ginger and pour over the pineapple. Sprinkle with brown sugar.

4. Broil the pineapple until tender and caramelized, about 12 minutes, basting every 3 to 4 minutes for even browning. Serve drizzled with the pan juices.

SAUTÉED APPLES WITH RAISINS AND BROWN SUGAR

HOW OFTEN DO ANY OF US HAVE THE TIME TO BAKE AN APPLE PIE? SO I SAY, WHY NOT MAKE THE FILLING AND SERVE IT WITH COOKIES AND ICE CREAM? ALMOND SHORTBREAD (PAGE 74) WOULD BE DIVINE HERE.

YIELD: 4 SERVINGS

¼ cup (½ stick) unsalted butter at room temperature

½ cup brown sugar, preferably Demerara (see page 8)

4 crisp apples, such as Gala, Crispin or Granny Smith, each cored and sliced into 8 wedges

¼ cup raisins

½ cup apple cider

½ teaspoon ground cinnamon

1. In a large skillet over high heat, melt the butter. Stir in the sugar and cook for 1 minute.

2. Arrange the apples in a single layer in the pan and scatter the raisins on top. Cook undisturbed for 6 minutes, or until the apples begin to caramelize.

3. Add the cider and cinnamon, bring to a boil, and cook for 1 minute.

4. Transfer the apples to a serving dish. Serve warm.

CHOCOLATE FONDUE

LEFTOVER FONDUE MAKES A GREAT SAUCE FOR ICE CREAM.
JUST REHEAT IT BEFORE SERVING.

YIELD: 4 TO 6 SERVINGS

½ pound unsweetened chocolate, chopped
1¼ cups brown sugar, preferably Sucanat
   (see page 8)
1 cup heavy cream
1 cinnamon stick, ground in a spice mill, or
   1 teaspoon ground cinnamon
½ teaspoon vanilla extract
Assorted fruits for dipping, such as sliced
   pears and apples, clementine segments,
   slices of crystallized ginger, and a selection
   of dried fruits

1. Fill a large saucepan with 1 inch of water and bring to a simmer over medium heat. In a medium stainless steel bowl, combine the chocolate and sugar. Set the bowl over the saucepan so it is suspended over the water (do not let the bowl touch the water). Alternately, use a double boiler. Stir the chocolate occasionally until smooth. Whisk in the cream, cinnamon, and vanilla. Whisk in 1 or 2 tablespoons of water if the mixture is too thick.

2. Pour the sauce into 4 to 6 warmed bowls and serve with a selection of fruits.

CARAMELIZED BANANAS WITH BLOOD ORANGE AND PISTACHIO

REGULAR ORANGE JUICE TASTES JUST AS GOOD AS BLOOD ORANGE JUICE HERE, BUT THE COLOR ISN'T NEARLY AS GORGEOUS.

YIELD: **4** SERVINGS

2 tablespoons roughly chopped
    unsalted pistachios
¼ cup brown sugar, preferably
    Demerara (see page 8)
3 tablespoons unsalted butter
4 ripe bananas, halved crosswise
2 plump dates, chopped
¼ cup freshly squeezed orange juice,
    preferably from a blood orange
Unsweetened yogurt or crème fraîche
    for serving

1. In a large skillet over medium heat, toast the pistachios for 1 minute, shaking the pan for even browning. Transfer to a plate to cool and set aside.

2. Return the skillet to high heat, add the sugar and butter, and cook, stirring, until the butter melts and the sugar dissolves, 1 to 2 minutes. Add the bananas and sauté for 1½ minutes. Turn the bananas over and sauté for 1½ minutes more. Add the dates and orange juice and bring to a boil. Cook for 30 seconds, then remove the pan from the heat.

3. Divide the bananas between 4 plates. Spoon the sauce over the bananas and sprinkle with toasted pistachios. Serve with yogurt or créme fraîche.

APRICOTS IN SPICED HONEY-WINE SYRUP

BLACK PEPPERCORNS, LEMON ZEST, AND FENNEL
CONTRIBUTE A WARM AND SPICY EDGE TO THIS
LUSCIOUS, SPEEDY COMPOTE.

YIELD: 4 TO 6 SERVINGS

1 pound dried apricots
1 cup dry white wine
⅔ cup honey
1 (3-inch) cinnamon stick
5 whole cloves
3 strips fresh lemon zest
1 teaspoon black peppercorns
½ teaspoon fennel seeds
Vanilla ice cream or lightly sweetened
    whipped cream for serving
Lightly toasted chopped nuts, such as cashews,
    almonds, or pistachios, for garnish
    (optional, see page 7)

1. In a pressure cooker over high heat, cover the apricots with the wine and 1 cup of water, and add the honey and cinnamon stick.

2. Wrap the cloves, lemon zest, peppercorns, and fennel seeds in cheesecloth, tie it closed with a piece of kitchen string, and add to the pressure cooker.

3. Lock the lid in place and bring to full pressure. Reduce the heat to low and cook for 7 minutes. Transfer the pot to the sink and run cold water over it to release the pressure.

4. Remove the cheesecloth bundle and cinnamon stick. Transfer the apricots and their liquid to a serving bowl and let cool slightly.

5. Serve warm with ice cream or whipped cream, sprinkled with toasted nuts, if desired.

APPLE CIDER COUSCOUS CAKE
WITH RED CURRANT GLAZE

HERE IS MY QUICK VERSION OF A TRADITIONAL MIDDLE
EASTERN JEWISH DESSERT—WONDERFUL WITH A BRACING
CUP OF YOUR FAVORITE BLACK OR HERBAL TEA.

YIELD: **4** SERVINGS

2½ cups apple cider

⅓ cup dried zante currants

⅛ teaspoon salt

1 cup couscous

1 cup sliced almonds, or roughly
    chopped walnuts or hazelnuts

1 (10-ounce) jar red currant preserves,
    or substitute apple cider jelly or any
    fruit preserve you like

1. Preheat the oven to 350°F.

2. In a medium saucepan over high heat, combine the cider, currants, and salt and bring to a boil. Stir in the couscous, cover the pot, and turn off the heat. Set aside until the couscous has absorbed all the liquid, about 10 minutes.

3. Transfer the couscous to a 8-inch springform pan or 9-inch pie plate and smooth the top with a spatula. Refrigerate until chilled, about 30 to 40 minutes.

4. Spread the nuts on a rimmed baking sheet and toast in the oven for 10 minutes. Transfer to a plate to cool.

5. Remove the sides of the springform pan (or invert the cake onto a plate if using a pie pan) and spread with preserves. If the preserves are too thick to spread, thin them with a little water. Press the toasted nuts into the cake and serve immediately.

GRAPEFRUIT COCKTAIL
WITH MASCARPONE AND
TOASTED ALMONDS

SPARKLING, ZESTY, SWEET-AND-SOUR GRAPEFRUIT
SUPREMES MAKE A REFRESHING WINTER DESSERT,
ESPECIALLY WHEN IT COMES BATHED IN ITS OWN SYRUP
WITH A DOLLOP OF CREAMY MASCARPONE CHEESE AND A
KISS OF BUTTER-TOASTED ALMONDS.

YIELD: **4** SERVINGS

5 large grapefruits
⅔ cup honey
1 vanilla bean, split lengthwise, pulp scraped with a knife
1 sprig fresh rosemary
1 tablespoon unsalted butter
½ cup sliced almonds
1 cup mascarpone cheese
¼ cup brown sugar, preferably
 Demerara (see page 8) or to taste

1. Cut 4 of the grapefruits in half along their equators and remove the segments cleanly with a small pairing or serrated knife, working over a bowl to collect any juice. Use a slotted spoon to transfer the sections to 4 wine glasses. Squeeze the membranes and skin to extract all the juice and strain the juice into a 2-cup measuring cup. You should have 2 cups of juice (if necessary, squeeze the juice from the remaining grapefruit and add some of that).

2. In a saucepan over high heat, combine the grapefruit juice, honey, vanilla pods and pulp, and rosemary and boil until the mixture is reduced to 1 cup, about 10 to 12 minutes.

3. Strain the syrup into a large glass measuring cup. Discard the vanilla pods and rosemary. Cool the syrup in the refrigerator for 10 to 15 minutes.

4. Meanwhile, in a large skillet over medium heat, melt the butter. Add the almonds and sauté for 3 to 5 minutes, stirring frequently for even browning. Transfer the almonds to a plate to cool.

5. Pour some of the cooled syrup over each serving, top with a dollop of mascarpone, and sprinkle with toasted almonds. Sprinkle each cocktail with 1 tablespoon of sugar, or to taste. Serve immediately.

INDEX

A

aïoli, vegetables, 52–54
almonds, toasted:
  grapefruit cocktail with
    mascarpone and, 284
  quinoa with Brussels
    sprouts, tempeh and, 182,
    184–85
almond shortbread cookies, 74
apple(s):
  green, and celery salad with
    walnuts and mustard vinai-
    grette, 246, 248
  with honey and cinnamon,
    212
  sautéed, with raisins and
    brown sugar, 278
apple cider:
  couscous cake with red cur-
    rant glaze, 283
  roasted winter squash with
    curry butter and, 190–91
apricots:
  roasted, in Riesling with
    black pepper, 142
  in spiced honey-wine syrup,
    282
arepas:
  giant, with aged Gouda,
    186–87
  pan-grilled Colombian corn
    cakes, 104, 107
artichokes:
  baby, with lemon vinaigrette,
    36, 39
  prepping, 23
arugula and white bean salad

with lemon dill vinaigrette,
  116, 119
Asian cucumber salad, 120–21
asparagus, roasted, with garlic,
  40–41
autumn desserts, 206–15
  apples with honey and cinna-
    mon, 212
  fresh fig crostini with ricotta
    and honey on toasted wal-
    nut bread, 209
  honey-roasted pears, 208
  maple chestnut mousse, 212
  new crop assorted nuts
    roasted in the shell with
    dried fruits, 209
  prunes in red wine and rose-
    mary syrup, 211
  roasted grapes with red
    wine, 208
  whole meal biscuits with
    cheeses and grapes, 214
autumn menus, 152–205
  baked eggs with escarole,
    onions, and Gruyère, 194,
    196
  barley risotto with golden
    beets, Swiss chard, and
    goat cheese, 172, 174
  black bean tostadas with
    cherry tomato salsa, 160,
    162–63
  braised pinto beans with del-
    icata squash, red wine, and
    tomatoes, 186, 188
  broccoli salad with ginger
    vinaigrette, 198–99

bulgur and buckwheat pilaf,
  202–3
chipotle roasted potatoes,
  194–95
fennel-cabbage slaw with
  raisins and apple, 172, 175
giant arepas with aged
  Gouda, 186–87
pad thai, 198, 200–201
pan-grilled radicchio salad
  with honey-balsamic glaze,
  176, 181
pasta with spicy cauliflower,
  chickpeas, and cherry
  tomatoes, 176, 178–79
pumpkin, pear, and fennel
  soup, 182–83
quinoa with Brussels sprouts,
  tempeh, and toasted
  almonds, 182, 184–85
radish, orange, and avocado
  salad, 160–61
red lentil and sweet potato
  curry with warm pita
  bread, 168–69
roasted winter squash with
  curry butter and apple
  cider, 190–91
romaine salad with sun-dried
  tomatoes and lemon-
  Parmesan dressing, 164–65
spicy red cabbage with
  cumin seeds and tomatoes,
  168, 171
stuffed greens with red bean
  and vegetables ragout, 190,
  192–93

tempeh and vegetable stew, 202, 204–5

warm mesclun salad with sherry vinaigrette and five-minute eggs, 154, 158–59

Wehani and wild rice stew with cremini mushrooms, winter squash, and kale, 164, 166–67

wild mushroom fricassee over farro, 154, 156–57

avocado:

chilled, soup with lime and jalapeño, 92, 96

garlic soup with tortillas, lime and, 28, 30–31

salad, radish, orange and, 160–61

slicing, 31

B

baking equipment, 10

bananas, caramelized, with blood orange and pistachio, 281

barley risotto with golden beets, Swiss chard, and goat cheese, 172, 174

beans:

braised pinto, with delicata squash, red wine, and tomatoes, 186, 188

canned, 6

red, and vegetables ragout, stuffed greens with, 190, 192–93

red, whole grain pasta with red wine, portobello ragout and, 224, 226–27

rice, peas and, 28–29

see also white beans

beets, golden, barley risotto with Swiss chard, goat cheese and, 172, 174

benriners (Asian mandolines), 10

berries, warm summer, with whipped crème fraîche, 148

Bibb lettuce and radish salad

with crème fraîche citronette, 20–21

biscuits, whole-meal, with cheeses and grapes, 214

black bean(s):

spicy, seared tofu with mango salsa and, 92, 94–95

tostadas with cherry tomato salsa, 160, 162–63

and zucchini quesadillas, 84–85

blenders, 10

blood orange, caramelized bananas with pistachio and, 281

blueberry(ies):

lemon-ricotta soufflé with, 140

in Muscat wine with vanilla ice cream, 144

-nectarine crisp, 143

borscht with caraway and dill, spring, 48, 50–51

bowls, 12

box graters, 12

broccoli:

salad with ginger vinaigrette, 198–99

sautéed, with lemon and garlic, 224–25

broccoli rabe:

with balsamic brown butter, 260, 265

bruschetta with ricotta and, 58–59

broth from trimmings, 41

bruschetta:

with broccoli rabe and ricotta, 58–59

with goat cheese, olives, tomatoes, and thyme, 108–9

Brussels sprouts, quinoa with tempeh, toasted almonds and, 182, 184–85

buckwheat:

and bulgur pilaf, 202–3

and vegetable pancakes with spicy yogurt sauce, 254, 258–59

bulgur wheat, 113

and buckwheat pilaf, 202–3

in tabbouleh, 32–33

buttermilk:

strata with portobello mushrooms and leeks, 40, 42

and strawberry soup, 76

C

cabbage:

crunchy, salad, 232, 237

and fennel slaw with raisins and apple, 172, 175

see also red cabbage

carrot(s):

and leek soup, 58, 61

maple roasted, 250, 253

and mint salad with currants, 24–25

spinach soup with basmati rice and, 44–45

cauliflower, spicy, pasta with chickpeas, cherry tomatoes and, 176, 178–79

celery and green apple salad with walnuts and mustard vinaigrette, 246, 248

champagne, strawberries in, 146

charmoula baked tempeh with vegetable couscous, 24, 26–27

cheese, grating, 6

cherries, roasted, in red wine, 77

chestnut mousse, maple, 212

chickpea(s):

pancakes with spicy tahini sauce, curried, 44, 46–47

pasta with spicy cauliflower, cherry tomatoes and, 176, 178–79

spicy summer bean salad with harissa vinaigrette and, 124–25

warm salad with shallots and red wine vinaigrette, 62, 65

chipotle:

roasted potatoes, 194–95

salsa, 87

chocolate fondue, 279

citrus, 6

coconut sweet potato soup with collard greens, spicy, 228, 230

coffee mills (electric), 12

colanders, 12

collard greens, spicy coconut sweet potato soup with, 228, 230–31

compote, maple rhubarb, with crystallized ginger, 76

cookies, almond shortbread, 74

corn:
    chilled tomato soup with shallots, cucumbers and, 98, 100–101
    fresh, polenta with sautéed cherry tomatoes, 124, 126–27
    and lentil salad with sweet peppers and coriander, 108, 110–11
    spicy, frittata with tomatoes and scallions, 88, 90–91

corn cakes, pan-grilled, Colombian (arepas), 104, 106

couscous:
    cake, apple cider, with red currant glaze, 283
    vegetable, charmoula baked tempeh with, 24, 26–27

cracked wheat, see bulgur wheat

crisps:
    blueberry-nectarine, 143
    rhubarb, 78

cucumber:
    Asian, salad, 120–21
    chilled tomato soup with shallots, corn and, 98, 100–101
    salad, 88–89
    soup with mint, chilled, 84, 86

currants, carrot mint salad with, 24–25

cutting boards, 12

D

dandelion greens, scrambled eggs with goat cheese and, 36, 38

dates, mango lime fool with, 73

delicata squash, see winter squash

desserts, see autumn desserts; spring desserts; summer desserts; winter desserts

dressings:
    crème fraîche citronette, Bibb lettuce and radish salad with, 20–21
    lemon-Parmesan, romaine salad with sun-dried tomatoes and, 164–65

Dutch ovens, 13

E

edamame, 132–33

eggs:
    baked, with escarole, onions, and Gruyère, 194, 196
    five-minute, warm mesclun salad with sherry vinaigrette and, 154, 158–59
    poached, with braised spring vegetables, grits, and chives, 20, 22–23
    scrambled, with dandelion greens and goat cheese, 36, 38
    sliced, warm green beans and new potatoes with grilled onions and, 98, 102
    see also frittatas

equipment, 10–15

F

farro, wild mushroom fricassee over, 154, 156–57

fennel:
    and cabbage slaw with raisins and apple, 172, 175
    soup, pumpkin, pear and, 182–83

figs:
    fresh, crostini with ricotta and honey on toasted walnut bread, 209
    roasted fresh, with raspberries, 147

fondue, chocolate, 279

food processors, 5, 12

frittatas:
    leek and potato, 242–43
    spicy corn, with tomatoes and scallions, 88, 90–91

fruit salad, summer, in herbed wine syrup, 144

G

garlic:
    and herb broth, Provençal, 238, 241
    mashed potatoes and parsnips, 232, 235
    pan-seared summer squash with mint and, 128, 131
    roasted asparagus with, 40–41
    sautéed broccoli with lemon and, 224–25
    soup with tortillas, avocado, and lime, 28, 30–31
    toasts, 91

glazes:
    honey-balsamic, pan-grilled radicchio salad with, 176, 181
    red currant, apple couscous cake with, 283

goat cheese:
    barley risotto with golden beets, Swiss chard and, 172, 174
    bruschetta with olives, tomatoes, thyme and, 108–9
    scrambled eggs with dandelion greens and, 36, 38
    and tomato strata, 260, 262

Gouda, aged, giant arepas with, 186–87

grains, 6

grapefruit cocktail with mascarpone and toasted almonds, 284

grapes:
 roasted, with red wine, 208
 whole meal biscuits with cheeses and, 214

green beans:
 spicy summer bean and chickpea salad with harissa vinaigrette, 124–25
 warm, and new potatoes with sliced eggs and grilled onions, 98, 102

greens, stuffed, with red bean and vegetables ragout, 190, 192–93

grits with braised spring vegetables, poached eggs, and chives, 20, 22–23

Gruyère:
 baked eggs with escarole, onions and, 194, 196
 grilled, and red onion sandwiches with grainy mustard, 266–67

H

herbed wine syrup, summer fruit salad in, 144

herbs, 6–7

honey:
 apples with cinnamon and, 212
 -balsamic glaze, pan-grilled radicchio salad with, 176, 181
 broiled pineapple with ginger, lime and, 276
 -roasted pears, 208
 warm, lemon curd over strawberries, 72
 -wine syrup, apricots in spiced, 282

hummus, lemon walnut, with warm pita, 32, 35

J

jalapeño, chilled avocado soup with lime and, 92, 96

jasmine rice, 228, 231

K

kale:
 sautéed, with red cabbage and caraway seeds, 220–21
 Wehani and wild rice stew with cremini mushrooms, winter squash and, 164, 166–67

kasha casserole with root vegetables and mushrooms, 246, 249

Kirby (pickling) cucumbers, 89

knives, 12

L

labneh (yogurt), 139

ladles, 12

leek(s):
 buttermilk strata with portobello mushrooms and, 40, 42
 and carrot soup, 58, 61
 cleaning, 61
 and potato frittata, 242–43
 three sisters stew with okra and, 104–5
 and turnip soup with potatoes and chard, 266, 268

lemon:
 curd, warm honey, over strawberries, 72
 and lentil soup with spinach, 254, 257
 -ricotta soufflé with blueberries, 140
 sautéed broccoli with garlic and, 224–25
 and walnut hummus with warm pita, 32, 35

lentil(s):
 and corn salad with sweet peppers and basil, 108, 110–11
 lemon, soup with spinach, 254, 257
 red, and sweet potato curry with warm pita bread, 168–69

lime:
 broiled pineapple with honey, ginger and, 276
 chilled avocado soup with jalapeño and, 92, 96
 garlic soup with tortillas, avocado and, 28, 30–31
 mango fool with dates, 73

M

mango:
 lime fool with dates, 73
 salsa, seared tofu with spicy black beans and, 92, 94–95

masa harina, 107

mascarpone, grapefruit cocktail with toasted almonds and, 284

measuring cups and spoons, 12–13

mesclun salad, warm, with sherry vinaigrette and five-minute eggs, 154, 158

millet pilaf, toasted, 270–71

mirin (rice wine), 135

Monterey Jack, pita pizza with green olives, chopped salad and, 128, 130–31

mortar and pestle, 13

mousse, maple chestnut, 212

mozzarella, smoked, warm white bean salad with sun-dried tomatoes and, 238–39

mushroom(s):
 cremini, Wehani and wild rice stew with winter squash, kale and, 164, 166–67
 gravy, hot open-faced tempeh sandwich with, 250, 252
 kasha casserole with root vegetables and, 246, 249
 porcini, and parsley risotto, 220, 222–23
 portobello, buttermilk strata with leeks and, 40, 42
 portobello ragout, whole grain pasta with red wine, red bean and, 224, 226–27
 wild, fricassee over farro, 154, 156–57

mustard greens, orzo with, 62–63

N

nectarine-blueberry crisp, 143
noodles:
  chilled soba, in dashi with
    tofu and shredded romaine,
    132, 134–35
  sesame, with tofu steaks and
    baby Asian greens, 66,
    68–69
nuts, new crop assorted,
  roasted in the shell with
  dried fruits, 209
nuts and seeds, 7

O

oils, storage of, 7
okra, three sisters stew with
  leeks and, 104–5
onions:
  baked eggs with escarole,
    Gruyère and, 194, 196
  cipollini, balsamic-roasted
    seitan with, 232, 234–35
  grilled, warm green beans
    and new potatoes with
    sliced eggs and, 98, 102
  red, grilled Gruyère and
    grainy mustard sandwiches
    with, 266–67
orange, radish, and avocado
  salad, 160–61
orzo with mustard greens,
  62–63

P

pad thai, 198, 200–201
pancakes:
  buckwheat vegetable, with
    spicy yogurt sauce, 254,
    258–59
  curried chickpea, with spicy
    tahini sauce, 44, 46–47
pantry tips, 6–8
Parmesan toasts, 52, 57
parsley:
  how to wash, 223
  and porcini mushroom
    risotto, 220, 222–23
parsnips, garlic mashed potatoes and, 232, 235

pasta:
  orzo with mustard greens,
    62–63
  with spicy cauliflower, chick-
    peas, and cherry tomatoes,
    176, 178–79
  whole grain, with red wine,
    red bean, and portobello
    ragout, 224, 226–27
  whole grain, with salsa cruda,
    116–17
peaches, roasted, with raspberry sauce and whipped
  Greek-style yogurt with
  cinnamon, 138–39
pear(s):
  honey-roasted, 208
  pumpkin, and fennel soup,
    182–83
peas, rice, and beans, 28–29
pea shoot and sprout salad,
  66, 69
peelers, 13
picadillo, 189
pilafs:
  bulgur and buckwheat, 202–3
  toasted millet, 270–71
pineapple, broiled, with honey,
  ginger, and lime, 276
pita pizza with green olives,
  Monterey Jack, and chopped
  salad, 128, 130–31
pizza stones, 13
polenta, fresh corn, with
  sautéed cherry tomatoes,
  124, 126–27
potatoes:
  chipotle roasted, 194–95
  garlic mashed, and parsnips,
    232, 235
  leek and turnip soup with
    chard and, 266, 268
  and leek frittata, 242–43
  warm green beans with
    sliced eggs, grilled onions
    and, 98, 102
  see also sweet potato
pots and pans, 13–14
pressure cookers, 15
Provençal garlic and herb
  broth, 238, 241

prunes in red wine and rosemary syrup, 211
pumpkin, pear, and fennel
  soup, 182–83

Q

quesadillas, black bean and
  zucchini, 84–85
queso fresco, 107
quinoa with Brussels sprouts,
  tempeh, and toasted
  almonds, 182, 184–85

R

radicchio:
  pan-grilled, salad with
    honey-balsamic glaze, 176,
    181
  salad, watercress and, 250–51
radish:
  and Bibb lettuce salad with
    crème fraîche citronette,
    20–21
  orange, and avocado salad,
    160–61
raspberries, roasted fresh
  figs with, 147
rasps, 14
ratatouille, tempeh, 112, 114
red cabbage:
  sautéed kale and caraway
    seeds with, 220–21
  spicy, with cumin seeds and
    tomatoes, 168, 171
red currant glaze, apple cider
  couscous cake with, 283
red lentil and sweet potato
  curry with warm pita bread,
  168–69
red wine:
  braised pinto beans with del-
    icata squash, tomatoes
    and, 186, 188
  roasted cherries in, 77
  roasted grapes with, 208
  and rosemary syrup, prunes
    in, 211
  whole grain pasta with red
    bean and portobello ragout
    and, 224, 226–27

rhubarb:
  crisp, 78
  maple, compote with crystallized ginger, 76
rice:
  basmati, spinach soup with carrots and, 44–45
  beans, peas and, 28–29
  jasmine, 228, 231
  Wehani and wild rice stew with cremini mushrooms, winter squash, and kale, 164, 166–67
ricotta:
  bruschetta with broccoli rabe and, 58–59
  fresh fig crostini with honey and, on toasted walnut bread, 209
  -lemon souffle with blueberries, 140
risotto, porcini mushroom and parsley, 220, 222–23
romaine, shredded, chilled soba noodles in dashi with tofu and, 132, 134–35
rubber spatulas, 14

S

salads:
  Asian cucumber, 120–21
  Bibb lettuce and radish, with crème citronette, 20–21
  broccoli, with ginger vinaigrette, 198–99
  carrot mint, with currants, 24–25
  chopped, pita pizza with green olives, Monterey Jack and, 128, 130–31
  crunchy cabbage, 232, 237
  cucumber, 88–89
  fennel cabbage slaw with raisins and apple, 172, 175
  green apple and celery, with walnuts and mustard vinaigrette, 246, 248
  lentil and corn, with sweet peppers and basil, 108, 110–11

  pan-grilled radicchio, with honey-balsamic glaze, 176, 181
  pea shoot and sprout, 66, 69
  radish, orange, and avocado, 160–61
  romaine, with red wine vinaigrette and Asiago toasts, 242, 245
  romaine, with sun-dried tomatoes and lemon-Parmesan dressing, 164–65
  spicy summer bean and chickpea, with harissa vinaigrette, 124–25
  warm chickpea, with shallots and red wine vinaigrette, 62, 65
  warm green beans and new potatoes with sliced eggs and grilled onions, 98, 102
  warm mesclun, with sherry vinaigrette and five-minute eggs, 154, 158–59
  warm white bean, with sun-dried tomatoes and smoked mozzarella, 238–39
  watercress and radicchio, 250–51
  white bean and arugula, with lemon dill vinaigrette, 116, 119
  white beans with mustard vinaigrette, 48–49
salad spinners, 14
salsas:
  cherry tomato, black bean tostadas with, 160, 162–63
  chipotle, 87
  cruda, whole grain pasta with, 116–17
  mango, seared tofu with spicy black beans and, 92, 94–95
salt and pepper, 7
sandwiches:
  grilled Gruyère and red onion, with grainy mustard, 266–67
  hot open-faced tempeh, with mushroom gravy, 250, 252

sauces:
  aïoli, 54
  balsamic brown butter, broccoli rabe with, 260, 265
  raspberry, with roasted peaches and whipped Greek-style yogurt with cinnamon, 138–39
  spicy tahini, curried chickpea pancakes with, 44, 46–47
  spicy yogurt, buckwheat vegetable pancakes with, 254, 258–59
  see also salsas
scallions, spicy corn frittata with tomatoes and, 88, 90–91
seitan, 163
  balsamic-roasted, with cipollini onions, 232, 234–35
shallots:
  chilled tomato soup with cucumbers, corn and, 98, 100–101
  warm chickpea salad with red wine vinaigrette and, 62, 65
sieves (strainers), 14
skillets, 14
snap peas, prepping, 58
soufflé with blueberries, lemon-ricotta, 140
soups:
  carrot leek, 58, 61
  chilled avocado, with lime and jalapeño, 92, 96
  chilled cucumber, with mint, 84, 87
  chilled soba noodles in dashi with tofu and shredded romaine, 132, 134–35
  chilled tomato, with shallots, cucumbers, and corn, 98, 100–101
  garlic, with tortillas, avocado, and lime, 28, 30–31
  leek and turnip, with potatoes and chard, 266, 268
  lemon lentil, with spinach, 254, 257
  Provençal garlic and herb broth, 238, 241

(soups continued)

pumpkin, pear, and fennel, 182–83

spicy coconut sweet potato, with collard greens, 228, 230

spinach, with basmati rice and carrots, 44–45

spring borscht with caraway and dill, 48, 50–51

strawberry buttermilk, 76

soy sauce, 7

spatulas, rubber, 14

spelt, *see* farro

spices, whole, 8

spinach:

lemon lentil soup with, 254, 257

soup with basmati rice and carrots, 44–45

spoons, 14

spring desserts, 70–79

almond shortbread cookies, 74

mango lime fool with dates, 73

maple rhubarb compote with crystallized ginger, 76

rhubarb crisp, 78

roasted cherries in red wine, 77

strawberry buttermilk soup, 76

warm honey lemon curd over strawberries, 72

spring menus, 18–69

baby artichokes with lemon vinaigrette, 36, 39

Bibb lettuce and radish salad with crème fraîche cit-ronette, 20–21

borscht with caraway and dill, 48, 50–51

braised spring vegetables with grits, poached eggs, and chives, 20, 22–23

bruschetta with broccoli rabe and ricotta, 58–59

buttermilk strata with porto-bello mushrooms and leeks, 40, 42

carrot leek soup, 58, 61

carrot mint salad with cur-rants, 24–25

charmoula baked tempeh with vegetable couscous, 24, 26–27

curried chickpea pancakes with spicy tahini sauce, 44, 46–47

garlic soup with tortillas, avo-cado, and lime, 28, 30–31

lemon walnut hummus with warm pita, 32, 35

orzo with mustard greens, 62–63

Parmesan toasts, 52, 57

pea shoot and sprout salad, 66, 69

rice, beans, and peas, 28–29

roasted asparagus with gar-lic, 40–41

scrambled eggs with dande-lion greens and goat cheese, 36, 38

sesame noodles with tofu steaks and baby Asian greens, 66, 68–69

spinach soup with basmati rice and carrots, 45

tabbouleh, 32–33

vegetables aïoli, 52–54

warm chickpea salad with shallots and red wine vinai-grette, 62, 65

white beans with mustard vinaigrette, 48–49

steamer insert, collapsible, 13

stews:

autumn tempeh and veg-etable, 202, 204–5

three sisters, with okra and leeks, 104–5

Wehani and wild rice, with cremini mushrooms, winter squash, and kale, 164, 166–67

winter vegetable, with maple-glazed tofu, 270, 272–73

stratas:

buttermilk, with portobello mushrooms and leeks, 40, 42

tomato goat cheese, 260, 262

strawberry(ies):

buttermilk soup, 76

in champagne, 146

warm honey lemon curd over, 72

sugar, types of, 8

summer desserts, 136–49

blueberries in Muscat wine with vanilla ice cream, 144

blueberry-nectarine crisp, 143

fruit salad in herbed wine syrup, 144

lemon-ricotta soufflé with blueberries, 140

roasted apricots in Riesling with black pepper, 142

roasted fresh figs with rasp-berries, 147

roasted peaches with rasp-berry sauce and whipped Greek-style yogurt with cinnamon, 138

strawberries in champagne, 146

warm summer berries with whipped crème fraîche, 148

watermelon with fleur de sel, 146

summer menus, 82–135

arepas: pan-grilled Colombian corn cakes, 104, 107

Asian cucumber salad, 120–21

black bean and zucchini quesadillas, 84–85

bruschetta with goat cheese, olives, tomatoes, and thyme, 108–9

chilled avocado soup with lime and jalapeño, 92, 96

chilled cucumber soup with mint, 84, 87

chilled soba noodles in dashi with tofu and shredded romaine, 132, 134–35

chilled tomato soup with shallots, cucumbers, and corn, 98, 100–101

cracked wheat, 112–13

cucumber salad, 88–89

edamame, 132–33

fresh corn polenta with sautéed cherry tomatoes, 124, 126–27

lentil and corn salad with sweet peppers and coriander, 108, 110–11

pan-seared summer squash with garlic and mint, 128, 131

pita pizza with green olives, Monterey Jack, and chopped salad, 128, 130–31

seared tofu with spicy black beans and mango salsa, 92, 94–95

spicy corn frittata with tomatoes and scallions, 88, 90–91

spicy summer bean and chickpea salad with harissa vinaigrette, 124–25

tempeh ratatouille, 112, 114

Thai-style tofu and vegetables in spicy coconut broth with jasmine rice, 120, 122–23

three sisters stew with okra and leeks, 104–5

warm green beans and new potatoes with sliced eggs and grilled onions, 98, 102

white bean and arugula salad with lemon dill vinaigrette, 116, 119

whole grain pasta with salsa cruda, 116–17

summer squash, pan-seared, with garlic and mint, 128, 131

sweet peppers, lentil and corn salad with coriander and, 108, 110–11

sweet potato:
and red lentil curry with warm pita bread, 168–69
spicy coconut, soup with collard greens, 228, 230–31

Swiss chard:
barley risotto with golden beets, goat cheese and, 172, 174
leek and turnip soup with potatoes and, 266, 268

T

tabbouleh, spring, 32–33

tempeh:
autumn, and vegetable stew, 202, 204–5
charmoula baked, with vegetable couscous, 24, 26–27
crispy, strips, 228, 231
hot open-faced, sandwich with mushroom gravy, 250, 252
quinoa with Brussels sprouts, toasted almonds and, 182, 184–85
ratatouille, 112, 114

Thai-style tofu and vegetables in spicy coconut broth with jasmine rice, 120, 122–23

toasts:
Asiago, 242, 245
garlic, 91
Parmesan, 52, 56

tofu:
chilled soba noodles in dashi with shredded romaine and, 132, 134–35
maple-glazed, winter vegetable stew with, 270, 272–73
seared, with spicy black beans and mango salsa, 92, 94–95
smoked, 201
steaks, sesame noodles with baby Asian greens and, 66, 68–69
Thai-style, and vegetables in spicy coconut broth with jasmine rice, 120, 122–23

tomato(es):
braised pinto beans with delicata squash, red wine and, 186, 188
bruschetta with goat cheese, olives, thyme and, 108–9
cherry, pasta with spicy cauliflower, chickpeas and, 176, 178–79
cherry tomato salsa, black bean tostadas with, 160, 162–63
chilled, soup with shallots, cucumbers, and corn, 98, 100–101
and goat cheese strata, 260, 262
sautéed cherry, fresh corn polenta with, 124, 126–27
spicy corn frittata with scallions and, 88, 90–91
spicy red cabbage with cumin seeds and, 168, 171
sun-dried, romaine salad with lemon-Parmesan dressing and, 164–65
sun-dried, warm white bean salad with smoked mozzarella and, 238–39

tongs, wooden, 14

tortillas, garlic soup with avocado, lime and, 28, 30–31

tostadas, black bean, with cherry tomato salsa, 160, 162–63

turnip and leek soup with potatoes and chard, 266, 268

V

vanilla beans, 8

vegetables:
and aïoli, 52–54
braised spring, with grits, poached eggs, and chives, 20, 22–23
ragout, stuffed greens with red bean and, 190, 192–93
root, kasha casserole with mushrooms and, 246, 249
stew, autumn tempeh and, 202, 204–5
and Thai-style tofu in spicy coconut broth with jasmine rice, 120, 122–23
winter, stew with maple-glazed tofu, 270, 272–73

vinaigrettes:
ginger, broccoli salad with, 198–99
harissa, spicy summer bean and chickpea salad with, 124–25

(vinaigrettes continued)
lemon, baby artichokes with, 36, 39
lemon dill, white bean and arugula salad with, 116, 119
mustard, green apple and celery salad with walnuts and, 246, 248
mustard, white beans with, 48–49
red wine, romaine salad with Asiago toasts and, 242, 245
red wine, warm chickpea salad with shallots and, 62, 65
sherry, warm mesclun salad with five-minute eggs and, 154, 158–59
vinegar, 8

W

walnuts:
green apple and celery salad with mustard vinaigrette and, 246, 248
and lemon hummus with warm pita, 32, 35
water, quality of, 8
watercress and radicchio salad, 250–51
watermelon with fleur de sel, 146
Wehani and wild rice stew with cremini mushrooms, winter squash, and kale, 164, 166–67
whisks, 14
white beans:
and arugula salad with lemon dill vinaigrette, 116, 119
with mustard vinaigrette, 48–49
warm, salad with sun-dried tomatoes and smoked mozzarella, 238–39
winter desserts, 274–85
apple cider couscous cake with red currant glaze, 283

apricots in spiced honey-wine syrup, 282
broiled pineapple with honey, ginger, and lime, 276
caramelized bananas with blood orange and pistachio, 281
chocolate fondue, 279
grapefruit cocktail with mascarpone and toasted almonds, 284
sautéed apples with raisins and brown sugar, 278
winter menus, 218–73
balsamic-roasted seitan with cipollini onions, 232, 234–35
broccoli rabe with balsamic brown butter, 260, 265
buckwheat vegetable pancakes with spicy yogurt sauce, 254, 258–59
crispy tempeh strips, 228, 231
crunchy cabbage salad, 232, 237
garlic mashed potatoes and parsnips, 232, 235
green apple and celery salad with walnuts and mustard vinaigrette, 246, 248
grilled Gruyère and red onion sandwiches with grainy mustard, 266–67
hot open-faced tempeh sandwich with mushroom gravy, 250, 252
kasha casserole with root vegetables and mushrooms, 246, 249
leek and potato frittata, 242–43
leek and turnip soup with potatoes and chard, 266, 268
lemon lentil soup with spinach, 254, 257
maple roasted carrots, 250, 254
porcini mushroom and pars-

ley risotto, 220, 222–23
Provençal garlic and herb broth, 238, 241
romaine salad with red wine vinaigrette and Asiago toasts, 242, 245
sautéed broccoli with lemon and garlic, 224–25
sautéed kale with red cabbage and caraway seeds, 220–21
spicy coconut sweet potato soup with collard greens, 228, 230
toasted millet pilaf, 270–71
tomato goat cheese strata, 260, 262
vegetable stew with maple-glazed tofu, 270, 272–73
warm white bean salad with sun-dried tomatoes and smoked mozzarella, 238–39
watercress and radicchio salad, 250–51
whole grain pasta with red wine, red bean, and portobello ragout, 224, 226–27
winter squash:
braised pinto beans with delicata squash, red wine, and tomatoes, 186, 188
roasted, with curry butter and apple cider, 190–91
Wehani and wild rice stew with cremini mushrooms, kale and, 164, 166–67
wooden tools, 12

Y

yogurt, whipped Greek-style with cinnamon, roasted peaches with raspberry sauce and, 136, 138–39

Z

zucchini and black bean quesadillas, 84–85